But You Must!

The Steve Lillis Story

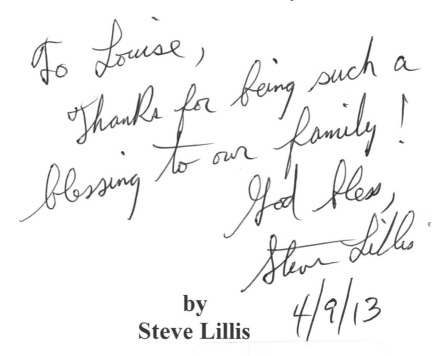

To Louise,
Thanks for being such a
blessing to our family!
God bless,
Steve Lillis
4/9/13

by
Steve Lillis

with Devr

D0733762

PUBLISHER
Gospel Trick Shot Ministries, Inc.

BUT YOU MUST!
The Steve Lillis Story

Copyright 2013 by Steve Lillis

Published by Gospel Trick Shot Ministries, Inc.
P.O. Box 313 Hawthorne, New Jersey 07507
Website: gospeltrickshot.org
Email: billiards12@hotmail.com

Scripture quotations are taken from the Holy Bible,
New Living Translation, copyright © 1996.
Used by permission of Tyndale House Publishers, Inc.,
Wheaton, Illinois 60189. All rights reserved.

Cover Design by Fred Robledo

Library of Congress Cataloging-in-Publication Data

Lillis, Steve

But You Must!
The Steve Lillis Story
ISBN-13: 978-1482312911
ISBN-10: 1482312913

Printed in the United States of America

Acknowledgement Page

I would like to acknowledge my Pastors John Minnema and Howard Van Dyk, Jr. of the Hawthorne Gospel Church who saw enough of Christ in me to stay with me during the dark days of my marital separation and beyond. I want to thank my dear friends and fellow Christian pool players Mike Massey and Tom "Dr. Cue" Rossman who spent many years investing and helping me not only with my pool game, but with life off of the pool table.

A special thanks to the Professional Writer's Group at William Paterson University in Wayne, New Jersey who inspired me to continue on with the project and helped lend some constructive criticism. A big thank you to the many who served on the Gospel Trick Shot Ministries, Inc. Board of Directors as they kept me on course with life by giving me the full counsel of God at each fork in the road.

And thanks to each significant person in the book who signed off on using their names so that they may share in my life journey in written form. A huge thank you to my dear friends and ministry partners, Fred and Devra Robledo, who hung in there with me for two years to help complete this project.

Most importantly, to my Lord and Savior Jesus Christ, I am eternally thankful for all you have allowed me to experience so that I may be used to help inspire others to find the Peace that passes all understanding.

"A Memoir"

My love for the sport of billiards began at a pool table in a bowling alley. The joy of playing was my fascination with watching the balls rolling along the felt toward their intended pockets.

As I got older, my focus changed. Joyful fascination turned into obsession when I began steering the balls toward the pockets for my own self serving profit and recognition.

Realizing the emptiness of my pursuit, I turned away from pool, vowing to never play again. However, God had a different plan...

To My Friends and Family...

*I share my story for the purpose of giving hope to others
who also struggle along life's journey...*

"O my people, listen to my teaching.

Open your ears to what I am saying,
for I will speak to you in a proverb.

I will tell of His power
and the mighty miracles He did.

So each generation can set its hope anew on God,
remembering His glorious miracles
and obeying His commands.

Then they will not be like their ancestors -
stubborn, rebellious, and unfaithful,
refusing to give their hearts to God."
(Psalm 78:1,2,7,8)

FOREWORD

The "road to victory" can often be a challenging maze of twists and turns with many potholes along the way. Pursuing a dream or perfecting a unique skill typically begins with an initial attraction and fascination to its primary focal point. As the journey continues, a person experiences personal relationships and valued resources which equip him or her to achieve the next level and beyond. The path to perfection in the chosen art form is normally traveled one step at a time, but sometimes occurs in giant leaps. Although triumphs typically keep moving a person forward, as life continues, perceived failures are often realized as ironic "successes in disguise."

The victory achieved in "But You Must!" is a parallel example to the road of life just described. The story is about my close friend, Steve Lillis, and the candid accounts of his personal journey with one of life's games (pocket billiards) and one of life's quests (a search for God).

As the story unfolds, Steve reveals his initial joy for the game of pool as he watches the spherical pool balls roll across the green felt. Many have experienced the draw into the sport of billiards via the scenic beauty of balls rolling and the sound of gentle clicks as they collide into one another's path. Even though Steve's story involves the game of pool, readers can place themselves into his experiences no matter what dreams their own lives have been drawn into. I have always felt that God allows each of us to individually experience a specific gift and that He gets our attention with whatever gift He has given us. "But You Must!" challenges readers to ponder their own personal gift along with their responsibilities to use it and for what end.

Steve follows his dream of becoming a professional pool player and, along the way, finds romantic love, serious challenges, and depression-ridden disappointments. The pitfalls of drugs, alcohol, strife, and gambling which often find residence in the world of pool create less than hospitable situations at every turn. In an attempt to find answers, Steve continues to ask the question, "What do you want me to do, Lord?" Although the answer does not come quickly, the answer does come.

As each of you "enjoy the roll" of your game in life, may you be inspired by Steve's story.

Rack Up A Victory in Your Game And Life!

>*Best Victories,*
>*Tom "Dr. Cue" Rossman*
>
>WPA World Artistic Pool Champion
>ESPN and World Masters Trick Shot Champion
>World Cup Of Trick Shots Champion (Team USA)
>Rack Up A Victory In Your Game And Life Missionary Outreach
>R.A.C.K. (Recreational Ambassadors For Christ's Kingdom) Vision

But You Must!

The Steve Lillis Story

INTRODUCTION

**"Wealth created by lying
is a vanishing mist and a deadly trap."**
(Proverbs 21:6)

"Come on." I say with a slurred voice acting more drunk than I really was. "Come on. At least give me the chance to win some of my money back. You're already up six hundred dollars."

My opponent looks toward his buddies as if to say, "Is he for real? This chump wants to keep playing only to let me steal more money from his pocket?"

Tonight is my first time in this bar and the 'pickins' are ripe for the harvesting. These pool players are obviously not accustomed to being hustled. Tonight's payday is going to be a good one.

In a seemingly honest tone my opponent replies, "Look bud, you've already lost your paycheck and you're drunk. Why don't you just go on home and sleep it off and cut your losses."

Like a fisherman who sees his bobber going up and down, I am confident of my catch. The game is on. My hustle has smoothly trapped my victim because he is mentally convinced of his skill to take me for every dollar in my pocket.

I begin my reeling technique of give and take. I allow him to win more often than not until little by little I begin to take a twenty here and a fifty there. As he begins to see his winnings decline, he is ready for my next hustle: "The double or nothing." Of course, I intentionally lose thereby priming him to accept my next drunken offer and then I begin reeling.

My pocket begins to again fill with my initial investment and then once I break even, I begin to pull out of my supposedly drunken stupor. My opponent is hooked. He thinks that he can beat me. Plus I have the advantage. His buddies are watching from the sidelines. At this point he must continue on to claim his ultimate victory. In my line of work, my opponent's pride is my best asset.

Suddenly, as when the fish feels the hook grab after he has bitten into the supposedly innocent worm, my opponent realizes that I can really play pool and his puffed chest begins to deflate. Now fear mixed with anger begins to drive him and he wriggles with defeat and humiliation as I begin running the table time after time. I am up $1600.

But I miscalculated.

All of a sudden I feel the push of cold sharp steel on my neck with my arms being helplessly pinned behind me. My opponent, now seething with rage, breathes into my ear, "You're a hustler and I'm going to kill you."

I begin to beg for mercy, "Okay, okay. I'm sorry. Please, just take your money out of my front pocket and I'll get out of here."

As if to make his threat good, he slowly slides the knife against my throat allowing me to feel the sharpness of the blade. When his blade runs out of neck to travel against, he places its point on my chin and uses it to persuasively turn my head so that he can look me straight in the eye.

With the conviction that there really is honor among thieves, he addresses me with authority, "You beat me fair and square, but you are a hustler. I am going to let you go to the bar and have a drink on me. Then, you are going to take all of your money and leave. If I ever see you around here again, I ... will ... kill ... you!"

12

He does not have to ask me twice. I quickly walk to the bar where the bartender is poised to immediately fill my order before a brawl breaks out. I down the drink in one swallow and bolt out of the door. Even to this day, some forty plus years later, I stay clear of that neck of the woods in northern New Jersey.

CHAPTER 1

"Tune your ears to wisdom,
and concentrate on understanding."
(Proverbs 2:2)

When I was a child, "I want to be a hustler" was not the answer I gave to those who asked "What do you want to be when you grow up?" Instead, my response was typical for many boys my age who were born in 1950. I wanted to be a professional baseball player.

How did my dream, which almost came true, turn into a nightmare? Like all of us, reality took a hold of me. I allowed the events in my life to lead me down a lonely, shady path. However, along the way, I discovered the ability of others to love and accept me despite my struggles and failures. Please join me as I share my journey of a life woven with triumph and tragedy.

Those with knowledge of our American history will note that I came on the scene about five years after World War II ended. In fact, my father was a World War II veteran, which was not unusual for boys my age. However, when it came to the "my dad's better than your dad" arguments with my friends, I had an edge because my dad had almost lost his life. He fought bravely in about a dozen naval battles and during one of those battles, 180 of his shipmates died during a series of kamikaze attacks. Of course, my dad did not share this story lightheartedly because he carried the scars on his heart for the death of his friends and sailors, but I was too young to comprehend the sorrowful reality of war. I was a boy with bragging rights.

My dad found romance after the service and married my mother, Eleanor Stetter. They stood with pride as the minister ended with the traditional "It is now my pleasure to introduce to you for the first time Mr. and Mrs. William Joseph Lillis." Four children later, with me being the oldest, their family was complete with two boys and two girls.

I began my life in my parent's home state of New York. My dad had grown up in the part of Long Island Queens where the Irish had been autonomous going back to the late 1800's. My mother, on the other hand, had come from a very German background in the Bronx.

A linguist would quickly ascertain my New York roots by listening to my speech patterns because I still speak with an Eastern twang. To those living in the southern, western, and mid-western states, I do not say "I 'saw' you." To their ears, I say "I 'sorer' you." Oh well, in the context of my sentences they know what I mean.

As my development approached school age, my parents moved our family across the Hudson River to northern New Jersey which was quickly defining itself as the preferred bedroom community for New York City workers. We settled into a little Dutch reformed town called Waldwick situated in Bergen County.

Growing up, I was just one of the boys on the block. We played kick the can, stick ball, touch football, street hockey, and other games gravitating over from New York City streets into the suburbs of New Jersey. Of course, the close proximity of great sports teams like the New York Yankees, the Brooklyn Dodgers, and the New York Giants, had a tremendous affect in cultivating our enthusiasm for the sports. As a result, like many boys and young men, I aspired to follow in the footsteps of these great team players.

Mixed together with my dream of becoming a professional baseball player was the reality of my education. Mimicking the little lamb in the nursery rhyme, I followed my friends to school. In addition to my public education, my parents made sure that I also received a spiritual education. Sunday mornings would find our family faithfully attending church. However, Sundays back in those days were different than Sundays today because stores used to be closed on this one special day of the week, making it impossible for me to go buy a licorice stick or pay my dime for a double scoop ice cream cone. Even most gas stations were not open, which held traveling to a minimum.

Of course, our culture back then was founded more predominately on the Bible so that this tradition of closing commerce down on Sundays stemmed back to the Ten Commandments. The fourth one reads, "Remember to observe the Sabbath day by keeping it holy. Six days a week are set apart for your daily duties and regular work, but the seventh day is a day of rest dedicated to the Lord your God."[1] Even if we question God on other things, we have to admit our inclination to comply with this commandment. Which one of us does not like to take a day off of work in order to enjoy a day of rest?

Even though we attended a Protestant church, my father actually came from a very traditional Irish Catholic background. My mother came from the opposite end of the religious spectrum. On her end, even the thought of worship was considered to be a bad influence. Wanting to accept an invitation to attend Catholic mass with her girlfriend, my mother was reprimanded for even asking. My grandmother forbade her with words like, "You don't need to go there. Religion is for weak people."

Although my mother was not allowed to attend church as a child, the Lord used this absence in her life to spark an early interest in her heart and she searched for the opportunity to meet God someday. Finally, upon marrying my dad, she attended Catholic mass for the first time and began to eagerly study the Bible. Needless to say, when the Billy Graham Crusade arrived at New York City's Madison Square Garden in 1957, she took my dad, my sister, and me in tow to hear this great man of God speak.

This was not an ordinary Billy Graham event. Rather, history records this as one of his greatest revival conferences. The Crusade had an operating budget amounting to an impressive $600,000. In addition, a significant percentage of Protestant churches in the city were brought in as supporters which is probably why my parents began attending a Protestant church soon thereafter.

From a media standpoint, the event was given extensive coverage. The New York Herald Tribune featured a front page column written personally by Billy Graham. ABC television broadcasted the Saturday evening services which drew in even more television viewers than the 500,000 people who actually attended the Crusade.

Martin Luther King, Jr. was also invited to the podium even though Billy Graham anticipated the controversy this would instigate among conservative whites. His willingness to welcome Dr. King, however, brought increased acceptance from the black community and, by the end of the event, almost 20 percent of the audience was black.

The Crusade opened on May 15th and closed on September 2nd with a giant rally in Times Square where more than 100,000 people packed the streets. The Billy Graham organization estimated the overall event attendance at more than 2 million people and reported 55,000 decisions for Christ. In addition, they received over 1.5 million follow-up letters.

Despite these staggering numbers, Billy Graham himself conceded defeat. Even with all of the enthusiasm and excitement surrounding the event, the long term impact within the city had been insignificant. Bible sales and new church memberships remained stagnant. Even though some ministers criticized Graham for his choice of venues, one rebuttal is worth our continued consideration, "What started in the Garden of Eden and reached its finest moment in the Garden of Gethsemane should be brought out of those gardens and into the present. And Madison Square Garden is as good a place as any for that."[2]

Returning to my story, Madison Square Garden was a good place to start for my parents because they turned their lives over to God that night. We were sitting way up in the balcony. At the end of the sermon, when the music started for people to come down to the platform and publicly announce their belief in Jesus Christ, thousands of people started drifting down the aisles.

As the audience was singing the great old hymn of the faith "Just As I Am," my mother grabbed my father's hand who in turn grabbed my sister's and my hand and I remember us walking down flights of stairs until we finally reached the stage. In my young mind, the descent seemed like it took forever, but our journey brought my parents to a point where they committed their lives to the Lord. My mother now knew that the God who she had wanted to meet as a child was now her God and friend Himself.

CHAPTER 2

"Teach your children to choose the right path,
and when they are older, they will remain upon it."
(Proverbs 22:6)

Watching a time lapse video is fun. Yesterday, an amazing video was featured on my computer's home page showing an 11 hour flight from San Francisco to Paris in just two minutes. This required the photographer to condense 5,576 miles into only 2,459 photos.[3]

Sharing my life story is, in many ways, like the photographer's job of capturing his journey on time lapse video. I must condense sixty plus years of my life experiences into a couple hundred pages in a manner that keeps you, the reader, entertained. Which stories do I choose? What life lessons do I share? How do I introduce myself? Where do I begin?

I know the answer to this last question. The year was 1960 and I was 10 years old. Two sports would begin to shape my identity at this young age. Baseball and billiards.

My father formed the foundation of my baseball skills by playing catch with me in the backyard. He was the pitcher and I was the catcher. Soon I found myself playing on the little league team where my performance drew praise from my coaches and cheers from my teammates. These accolades served to build my confidence and my desire to play baseball grew even more. However, my goal to actually enter professional baseball came from the role model of a player who attended our church.

After the Billy Graham Crusade, my parents began attending Grace Church in Ridgewood, New Jersey. I enjoyed the Sunday school classes, but having to sit through the church services brings back memories of my being bored stiff.

In church, I was that fidgety kid who was learning the art of speed reading through the hymnal, testing the structural integrity of the pews by means of foot pressure, and autographing my artwork on every available slip of paper in sight. Due to my distracted behavior, my parents would sometimes allow me to go sit in the car until after the service.

One Sunday morning I had no interest in going to the car. Bobby Richardson, the professional baseball player, had taken a seat a few pews ahead of our family. My attention suddenly became riveted on this man who was the image of what I wanted to become.

Robert Clinton "Bobby" Richardson was the second baseman for the New York Yankees from 1955 through 1966. Before he retired, he would become an eight times All-Star, become the World Series Champion three times, win the Gold Glove Award five times, and be awarded the 1960 World Series MVP.[4]

Week after week I admired this baseball legend who was sitting less than a pitcher's mound away from me. I would see him in church and then I would go home and see him playing second base on a televised Sunday baseball game. He would even go to church on game days! During his baseball career he became known as a "workhorse" because he rarely missed a game. I can attest to the fact that not only did he rarely miss a game, but he rarely missed church. Bobby Richardson was a devout Christian and, even today, he travels across the country using his baseball career as his home base for sharing the Gospel with others.

My proximity to this baseball star became very significant in my life. I was already involved with sports and I considered myself a "Christian" (after all, I did like Sunday school). In my young mind, I was already on the way to becoming a professional baseball player like Bobby. And he was "Bobby" to me because he used to take our youth group out and hit fly balls to us. Afterwards, he taught us about Jesus. He explained that we were always a winner in God's sight even when we lost. This admonition really stuck with me because Bobby Richardson was the winner of the 1960 World Series Most Valued Player Award. However, this MVP recognition came with the distinction of him being the only World Series MVP ever to be selected from the *losing* team. Bobby Richardson became the most valued player even though he was on the losing team. Talk about a life lesson!

And where was Bobby sitting the Sunday after receiving this award and losing to the Pittsburgh Pirates? He was faithfully sitting in church just a few pews ahead of my family.

As my dedication to the sport of baseball continued to grow, I remember praying every time I got up to bat, "God, I just want to play for you and I want to be the best baseball player that I can be." I wanted to mirror Bobby Richardson and I was actually on the pathway to a successful career in baseball until I allowed events in my life to steer me elsewhere.

Before we jump ahead, do you remember when I said, "Two sports shaped my identity early on in my life?" Baseball was one and billiards, or pool, was the other. Returning to when I was 10 years old, I joined a bowling league. Even though I was a good baseball player, I was a lousy bowler. I guess I excelled at sports where I could use a wooden stick to strike at a ball. A bat in baseball and a cue in billiards.

Because I was bored with the game of bowling, I would slip away in between frames to play on a little coin operated pool table toward the back of the bowling alley. I dropped in my coin, hit the balls, (pocketing most of them on my first try), and then ran back to take my turn at bowling. Over a period of time, I discovered that not only did I enjoy pool, but I was good at it.

This discovery led to my request for a pool table. The year was 1961 and I had been asking my parents for a pool table sporadically for many months. However, with Christmas right around the corner, placing such a large item on my wish list never occurred to me. I was asking for reasonable things like a new baseball glove, a new baseball bat, or maybe even a "Johnny Reb Cannon" or a "Great Garloo" which were the popular toys that ycar. "Ken," the fictional boyfriend of toy doll "Barbie," was also introduced in 1961, but he was not on my list. I was interested in sports. Girls, boys, and the whole dating scene were not even on my radar screen yet.

However, "Ken" would have been the perfect gift for either of my two sisters. Maybe he was, I don't remember. My memory recalls the scene of my sisters each surrounded by over two dozen presents early Christmas morning and I only had a couple of small packages sitting in front of me. My parents were acting as if nothing was wrong. As my sisters continued to open gift after gift after gift, I continued to spiral into self pity. Obviously, my parents loved my two siblings more than they did me.

Of course my mother's comments were not helping. "Ohhhhh....Poor Stephen," (which was my given name, but I liked my friends to call me Steve), "he didn't get many Christmas presents this year." "He must have been a bad boy." "His stocking must be full of coal." She intentionally teased me until my strength to hold back the tears was about to weaken and then she exclaimed, "Wait a minute! Where's Dad? I think I heard him go down to the basement. Let's go find him."

I had not noticed my father's absence. As I would soon discover, he was down in the basement with the flood lights on and the cameras rolling to catch the expression on my downtrodden face when I descended the steps and caught a glimpse of my very own pool table! A brand new Sears 4'x8' pool table with glistening shiny billiard balls and a playfield of green felt.

Joyously, I grabbed the cue stick which was lying on the table and I racked the balls and pocketed the balls, racked the balls again and pocketed the balls again. I ran racks of balls throughout the remainder of Christmas Day. My mother must have served me breakfast, lunch, and dinner at the pool table because I do not remember leaving my precious gift for the next eight to ten hours.

Thus began my adventure into pool. As the years progressed, when I was not playing the team sport of baseball on the green field of grass, I was playing the individual sport of billiards on the green field of cloth. For the record, I was good.

CHAPTER 3

"It is senseless to pay tuition
to educate a fool who has no heart for wisdom."
(Proverbs 17:16)

Opportunity in the life of one person can produce trauma in the life of another. I learned this lesson when I was in the eighth grade. My dad was offered an opportunity of a higher paying position which he made the decision to accept. This occupational change required our family to move to the much larger township of Wayne, New Jersey. Did my dad know that his acceptance of this job offer would traumatically alter the course of my life causing me to go astray from my childhood upbringing? Obviously not. However, this move during my formative teen years led into what was really the opening chapter of my life story.

We did not just move away from my little hometown of Waldwick. We moved away from a community where I was the star baseball player, probably the best athlete in town. We moved away from my church where I was actively involved and where I had a professional baseball player as a role model to follow. We moved away from my friends and school where I was excelling as a student. We moved away from my comfort zone into what would soon prove to be a danger zone.

I was about 14 years old at the time. Given my interest in athletics, my first line of action was to go out for sports in my new school. Being new to Wayne, nobody knew me like they did in my previous hometown. I had to prove all over again my worthiness to be on their team.

This led to a lot of peer pressure because many of the athletes in this big town had grown up together and had played sports among themselves for years. Everybody already knew each other's athletic capabilities and who was going to play what position.

Now I entered the scene as the new kid on the block. To their dismay, I tried out for their team and proved my credibility as a good athlete. The coaches saw my talent and placed me on the roster ahead of other regular players on the team. Understandably, resentment naturally began to build up and I began to feel different about myself.

Among my athletic peers I was not wanted. I was rejected. I was not liked. Bitterness began to build up and I started to hang out with new friends who were welcoming me into their circle. My new crowd was not into athletics, though. Their pastime included smoking, drinking, and drugs.

As a result, I developed a schizophrenic lifestyle. When playing sports, I was the healthy athlete who my teammates begrudgingly acknowledged, but did not accept as their friend. When not playing sports, I was the wasted teenager who my friends willingly accepted because I took part in their unhealthy lifestyle of alcohol, drugs, and gambling. Day to day life was forcing me to choose between my enjoyment of competing in sports and my desire to be embraced by friends.

Of course, my mother and father noticed my involvement with the wrong crowd and they naturally became concerned. Tension grew within the household especially on Sundays when I was expected to attend church with the family. My increasing rebellion resulted in my decision to stop going to church. This, in turn, stopped my conversations with God. It was almost as if my last words to Him were, "Thanks for the ride, God, but I will take over from here."

With my ties to family and God now cut as far as I was concerned, I struck out on my own. This was my junior year in high school and I was 16 years old. Not only was I an accomplished athlete, but I had also developed excellent skills playing the game of pool after five years spent in our basement running the table rack after rack.

In 1961, the hit movie "The Hustler" was released starring Jackie Gleason as Minnesota Fats and Paul Newman as Eddie Felson. Because the storyline was written with such believability, viewers thought that Minnesota Fats and Eddie Felson were real people who had experienced the true life adventures portrayed in the movie. For the record, they were just fictional characters until a pool player named Rudolf Wanderone claimed to be the player used by the movie directors to cast Minnesota Fats. This false claim proved to make Rudolf, thereafter known as Minnesota Fats, one of the most famous pool playing names in history.

Pool was in a boom cycle because of "The Hustler" and billiard rooms were sprouting up all over the country. More importantly to my life story, the laws in 1966 allowed 16 year old patrons into pool rooms and I was a 16 year old boy with the experience of a smoking, drinking, gambling, pool playing man.

When I walked into my very first pool room, I felt at home. I blended in. As I watched players like Jack Colavito and Pat Fleming, I began to think, "You know what? I can do this. I can play as good as them ... if not better." Those thoughts were the start of what would soon become my unhealthy addiction to pool.

With my confidence on the upswing, I started to frequent pool halls where I quickly learned the gambling aspects of the sport. Little by little, I began to win more than I lost. As a high school student involved with friends who "drink and chew and hang around with girls who do," this added income was an incentive to continue.

I was a senior and my grades were slipping. However, my involvement in school athletics was still in full swing and accompanied by many accomplishments. My repertoire of sports included baseball, soccer, basketball, and hockey. I was a second team all-county baseball player and honorable mention all-county soccer player so that I was not only one of the best in my town, but I was one of the best in the whole county. Yet I had no clue what I was going to do with my life after high school.

Even though I was uncertain of my future, our government had a plan. The Vietnam War draft was in place in 1968 and I became eligible for military service upon graduation. Despite my rebellious attitude toward authority, my options were slim. I could either submit to our government and be drafted or I could submit to my father who wanted me to attend college and request a draft deferral for educational reasons.

Without any direction in my life except for wanting to play pool and become a professional baseball player, my father gave a very convincing argument for me to pursue an electrical engineering degree at Georgia Tech. Upon hearing his offer to pay my school and lodging expenses, I chose his road to education.

My decision to attend Georgia Tech was really doomed from the start because the dream to become an electrical engineer was my dad's dream, not mine. My father meant well. He saw my life heading down the wrong track and he was attempting to steer me in another direction. However, just like a compass always points north, once I arrived at Georgia Tech in the fall of 1968, my internal direction finder gravitated to the pool room. Pool provided an immediate return on my investment whereas the reward for all of my classroom studies was somewhere out there in the distant future. With my talent for winning, I always had plenty of cash in my pocket to feed my appetite for good food, fun parties, and pretty girls. As a result, I started to cut classes and my grades began to drop. A thin thread was offering itself to me, but I was not making any effort to hold on.

At the end of my second semester, I became very sick due to my nightlife of partying and playing pool. Discovering my condition, my father got on a plane and flew down to help his fledgling son. He not only nursed me back to health, but he gained permission from the dean for me to take incompletes because I had been sick during final exams. In addition, he negotiated for me to take make-up exams after I had recuperated in order to salvage whatever grades were salvageable. I squeaked through my first year of college with a 2.01 average.

With summer break at hand, my father took me home and stated the obvious. "Son, I'm not sending you back to Georgia Tech next semester. You clearly can't handle the independence of living on your own. Next semester you can go to school locally."

This plan was fine with me except for his choice of another top engineering school in the northeast called Stevens Institute of Technology located nearby in Hoboken, New Jersey. When the next semester rolled around, I found myself repeating the same lifestyle as I had lived the year before. I only lasted one semester at this school.

My tendency to drop out of school would have most likely continued if the lottery had not replaced the draft. On December

1, 1969, the Selective Service System of the United States held a lottery to determine the order of draft, or induction, into the Army for the Vietnam War. Without going into the particulars of this new system, the importance to my story was my assigned number. The highest draft number called for induction from the 1969 lottery was 195 and my number was 305.[5] The chances of my getting drafted were slim to none.

The lottery was therefore my ticket out of school. My parents were still allowing me to live at home while I pursued my schooling, but I had not recognized this cause and effect condition. Upon announcing my intention to quit school and spend my time playing pool, my dad's tough love reaction triggered the repercussions of my decision. He responded, "No. You are not going to live in this house and just play pool. If you want to continue living here, then you're going to have to go out and work at a legitimate job. And just to be clear, playing pool is not a legitimate job."

Without any place to go, I begrudgingly accepted a position at Allied Chemical which my mother helped me find. In other words, I was a typical young person who was all "bark" that I was going to go out and do my own thing with no "bite" to actually go out and do it.

I remained muzzled at Allied Chemical for the next year and a half. Aside from playing pool, I started playing baseball again and I enrolled in some philosophy courses at a nearby college. This last activity allowed me to hang around with girls my age and be a part of the alluring lifestyle to which I had become accustomed. Just like in high school, I was leading a double life. During the day I worked at my "legitimate job" to please my parents and at night I partied and played pool to please myself.

Because my dating habits were unacceptable to display among the family circle of my younger brother and sisters, my father once again confronted me with another set of challenging words. "Son, you are going to either change your lifestyle or leave the house." With my circumstances now changed, I bit back, "No problem. My friends have wanted me to come live with them and I'm making plenty of money playing pool. I'll be out by the weekend."

I quit my job and moved into a log cabin with friends. My wealth of accumulated pool winnings allowed me to avoid work for a year. With no one to hold me accountable, I basically dropped out of society and did my own thing. Drugs. Alcohol. Parties. Girls.

Even though Disneyland is the "Happiest Place on Earth," a person visiting on a short vacation would soon become bored if he or she had to spend every day of the year there. In the same manner, my once alluring lifestyle had turned into a life without satisfaction or excitement. This boredom motivated me to find a job at a local pool room called Verona Billiards where I became the house manager. I was finally growing up. Or was I?

CHAPTER 4

"People ruin their lives by their own foolishness
and then are angry at the Lord."
(Proverbs 19:3)

Working at Verona Billiards allowed me to practice my craft. Up until now, playing pool had been an income producing hobby. With some serious study, my billiard skills could be developed into a business. A shady business admittedly, but a pursuit which would fill my pockets regularly with large sums of money. I became a professional hustler.

During the day, I would manage the affairs of the pool room. At night, I would frequent bars in the surrounding counties as a hustler disguised as a simpleton pool player. My staff was a group of gambling friends who eagerly accepted a position in this entrepreneurial venture.

For those unfamiliar with the cunnings and techniques of a hustler, allow me to briefly explain so that you will not unwisely fall victim to their escapades. Sometimes a hustler travels alone and lures in his prey similar to my experience in the opening pages of this book. Of course, not every dupe has the courage for revenge like that opponent demonstrated. If they did, the occupation of hustling would have lost its romanticism long ago.

However, because hustling can be a high risk occupation as my experience showed, many hustlers travel with an entourage of fellow gamblers who are just as adept at performing on the stage of deception. For the most part, I traveled with a band of these actors and actresses. Their first role was to go stake out places and find people who gambled on a pool table.

I would like to take a moment to linger on the importance of this last statement. As a hustler, I had to find people who were willing to gamble. In other words, not every pool player is a gambler willing to sacrifice the integrity of the game. Some pool players are honest, upright individuals who are perfecting their skills within a game requiring as much talent, dedication, and excellence as in many of our more popular sports.

If the sport of professional billiards reported the player stats like in other traditional sports, the viewing public might be surprised at the proficiency level achieved by these top players. Acclaimed to be the greatest basketball player of all times, Michael Jordan held a career field goal percentage of 49.7%. His ball made it into the hoop 49.7 times out of every 100 balls thrown. This is a great accomplishment in basketball, but a very humiliating stat to hold if you are a pool player.

Perfection is essential to succeed on the pool table. If your stat is not close to 100%, meaning that 100 out of 100 balls you shoot make it into the pocket, your chances of losing the game have just increased exponentially upon your first miss. Within a professional setting, one miss means that the opponent stepping up to the table will most likely win.

A pool player's drive for perfection motivates him or her to keep picking up the cue stick in order to shoot again. Within his or her heart and soul is the desire to achieve perfection. Of course, a lot of shots will be missed. However, for every successful shot, a player experiences oneness with the universe of physics and mathematics. Watching the linear reaction of balls rolling across the table to the desired pocket destination has a beauty and fascination which lures a player back to the pool table over and over again.

Even though many of these pool enthusiasts limit their play to individual practice or legitimate competitive arenas through local leagues and tournaments, some players prefer to also dabble in the gambling side of the sport. My crew's job was to find those players who felt confident enough in their skills to place money on the table.

Hustlers exist because the nature of man is to take advantage of the perceived weakness of another. Therefore, in order for me to play the part, my actions had to allow my opponent to feel stronger than me. One could conjecture that I encouraged others to feel good about themselves.

Because I was heavily into drugs and alcohol, the art of looking vulnerable came easy. I did not look weak physically because I still worked out every day. Despite my buff appearance, however, I held the etchings of being a marijuana, acid, speed, cocaine, alcohol, and cigarette user within the folds of my skin. This put my opponents off guard because they assumed that I was a "good for nothing" roamer who spent no time perfecting his game so that even though I may be lucky and get a few runs of pocketed balls here and there, I was by no means accomplished enough to run the table efficiently over the long haul.

Sadly, people fell for my hustle most of the time. Every one of us knows what a hustler does and yet whether it is in the game of pool or another situation, most of us can remember a time when they were a victim to such deception. A friend shared with me a story about losing twenty dollars at the gas pump many years ago. A man came up and said, "I'm going up to pay for my car over there on Number 4, I'd be happy to save you the walk and pay for yours here on Number 2." My friend never saw his twenty dollar bill or this kindly gentleman again.

However, the gas station hustler looked respectable and clean cut. He fit the profile of being trustworthy in order to successfully pull off his scam. My hustling techniques required my appearance to be dense and inconsistent. Of course I had to show some skill in playing the game or my opponent would not have had any interest in playing at the same table with me. He had his integrity too!

Whether I was playing the part of an alcoholic, a drug addict, a hippy acid user, or a cool hustler, my friends and I entered bars and gambled our reputations for money. Since I was the person actually playing pool and taking the money, I was the one taking the brunt of the repercussions. My partners in crime earned their cut by finding the venues, anonymously creating competitive interest, taking side bets, and heckling challenges from the crowd. They were not the target of attack upon leaving the bar by those who had been hustled. I was. An observer might have questioned whether my "dense" act was really an act because it took me longer than it should have to recognize the high risk to my personal health and safety.

Looking back, I am blessed to be alive given the number of duped victims who were waiting out in the parking lot to jump me or even shoot me. I actually came to consider the police as my friend because of the many times a bar owner called them to escort me out before a brawl erupted. And, of course, let's not forget the knife sliding across my throat incident.

With probably the first hint of maturity in my life, I thought to myself, "Maybe I shouldn't hustle anymore. Maybe I should just become the best pool player in the world." A strikingly familiar fantasy echoing from my childhood days of wanting to be the best baseball player in the world.

"What did happen to your baseball career?" some may be asking. "After all, you were a second team all-county baseball player in high school."

My answer goes back to when I worked at Allied Chemical. I had continued my involvement with baseball and, in fact, I played semi-pro ball. The scouts had been watching my performance and the Philadelphia Phillies were interested in signing me. The pitcher from my team had already signed a professional contract, but before his dream became a reality, he was killed in a car wreck while driving home from a bar where a bunch of us would drink together after hours.

My dream almost became a reality, too, until it was killed in a suicide squeeze play at home plate during a semi-pro game. The summer was 1970 and I was the catcher. The player on third base began running to home plate just as the batter bunted the ball straight up into the air. I jumped up to retrieve the ball, but my feet never returned to the ground because the player coming down from third base scored a run by hitting me like a linebacker. Knocked back ten feet to the backstop, I was down for the count. The resulting dislocation of various discs in my back ended my baseball career.

Who had terminated my baseball career? None other than my childhood baseball rival, Jack Van Yperen. He had been in my church youth group back at Grace Church in Ridgewood, New Jersey, where New York Yankee's Bobby Richardson had significantly influenced my life. Jack and I had both fallen in love with baseball. We had both dreamed of playing professional ball

32

and we had both become the top athletes in our respective home towns. Jack had played in Ridgewood and I had played in Waldwick. Now, years later, he inadvertently bowled me down like I was a bowling pin.

Looking back on this moment, I ponder God's choice of Jack as the instrument to effectively end my baseball career. Not only had we both sought the privilege to play baseball for God as boyhood friends, but his older brother, Dick, had been my first youth group leader who had significantly nurtured my early desire to believe. Now, years later, my life had taken a completely different turn.

After this incident, I turned even angrier at God, blaming Him for taking away my dream of pursuing a baseball career. In total rebellion now, I said, "Well, if my baseball career is over, I'm just going to play pool. And nobody can stop me from playing pool." And nobody did stop me. For the next two years I hustled my way through all of the bars in the territory until one day I realized that I could become a professional pool player.

CHAPTER 5

"A cheerful heart is good medicine,
but a broken spirit saps a person's strength."
(Proverbs 17:22)

The year was 1973 when I made the decision to *turn* professional. I specifically chose to use the word "turn" because I had reached a turning point in my life. My plan to pursue a professional career in pool motivated my effort to turn away from my dangerous involvement with the underground world of hustling.

My relationship status had changed. I was married now to a girl named Patti. We had met a few years earlier, and as the old saying goes, "opposites attract." While Patti steered clear of drugs and held down a good job, I conversely continued in my substance abuse and pool hustling career. Ours was not exactly the perfect marriage, but Patti was always very supportive and did not judge me for who I had become.

I remember when I told her about my decision to enter my first professional tournament where I would be competing against some of the best players in the sport. She encouraged me with a smile and said, "You can do this, hon." With her support and my determination to win, I entered my first professional "Straight Pool" tournament.

Straight Pool, also called "14.1 Continuous" or simply "14.1" is a pocket billiards discipline and was the dominant game of championship competition through the 1970's and early 1980's. As the sport of pool has evolved, this game has been overtaken by faster playing games such as nine-ball and eight-ball. However, Straight Pool is the classic game from the history of billiards. In fact, the game gained increasing popularity in the 1960's when it was immortalized in the 1961 film "The Hustler."

The basic rules of Straight Pool are simple. The object is to reach a set number of points (typically 100 or more) determined by agreement before the game. Each point represents a pocketed ball so that the player who pockets 100 balls before his opponent pockets 100 balls is the winner. A missed ball in the pocket results in loss of turn. Fouls result in loss of turn and loss of point.

In my very first professional match, I was dominated by one of the best Straight Pool players named Pete Margo. My participation in the game involved only two shots because Pete ran 116 straight balls into the pockets and the game was only to 125. He sat me in my chair for an hour straight as he ran 116 balls in a row. At the end of the match, he shook my hand, looked me in the eye, and said, "Welcome to the big leagues kid."

After such a humiliating loss, I realized my need for some serious pool practice in order to get my game to a level where I could compete against someone like Pete. For the next few years, 1973 to 1975, I began to dedicate myself to playing pool. Without regard to whether the person was a gambler or not, I searched out any skillful player who would challenge me. My game began to significantly improve and I was beginning to make a name for myself. In fact, most professional pool players are dubbed with a nickname and, in 1975, Mike Ash at the Hi Cue Billiard Lounge in Elizabeth, New Jersey, gave me mine. Because I was quick to jump up to the table and I was a lively player choosing unpredictable shot attempts, Mike referred to me as "Leapin" Lillis for media hype reasons and the name stuck.

With newfound confidence, I once again entered a professional pool tournament. Approximately ten world champions were playing in this event and I surprised them all by taking fourth place. Under my breath I now retorted, "Yeah! Welcome to the big leagues and I'm one of you now!" My ego had been fed a healthy dose of pride which fueled my already egotistical mannerisms. I was immune from caring about what others thought and I was completely content to live life on my own terms.

Or so I thought. I soon discovered that underneath my self sufficient armor was a vulnerable man who was sensitive to the opinion of others.

The occasion was a $5000 winner take all challenge match in which I was pitted against another professional player. The media was covering this event to verify whether my fourth place victory was based on skill or whether it was the luck of having a good run. The arena was set apart behind a big curtain with room for about 200 attendees who were paying $5.00 each to watch the match.

Of course I could care less about the audience because I had always played pool for my own self serving purpose. However, something happened inside of me when I saw my parents, my brother, and one of my sisters walk in and take their seats among the spectators. I had made little to no contact with my family in recent years.

Why were they there? From as far back as high school they had never supported my pool playing career. Why would they begin to support me now? Had my parents been following my pool career? Did my parents really care? Had my parents come to see me succeed in my beloved sport? After causing them so much grief, had I misinterpreted their interest in my life due to my rebellion of wanting to do things my way? Were they saying, "We love you, Son. We're here with you if this is what you are choosing?"

The realization that my family might actually love me and care about me unconditionally spurred an inner desire to prove my worthiness to them and be accepted back within the fold. I had to win this match. If I won, then I could win back the respect of my family. If I lost, then I would prove myself to be a continued failure in their eyes or so I thought.

The $5000 prize fund was no longer important. My identity as a person was at stake. This match was going to determine whether I could be loved and whether I could love. And I lost.

Of course my parents came up afterwards and congratulated me on a game well played, but in my heart, I had proven myself to be a miserable failure. I was not only unworthy to be my parent's son, but I was unworthy to even be on the professional side of pool. My dreams on both a personal level and career level had been shattered. I had no desire to move forward in life and I spent the next seven months hidden away in my apartment unwilling to leave.

What caused my depression? As with many of us who struggle with sadness, emptiness, and despair, I cannot really give a clear cut reason. A combination of genetic, psychological, and environmental factors is often involved in the onset of depression, and I could point to some of each as a reason if I had to defend my condition.

My wife caringly scheduled counseling appointments, but the counselor turned the situation around and blamed her for my plight. He accused her of enabling my habits and addictive lifestyle. Obviously his advice did not help me and probably caused Patti some depressed feelings of her own. Understandably, our outings to seek therapy ended.

The positive side to my retreat from society was my inaccessibility to cigarettes, alcohol, and drugs, thereby allowing my body to cleanse itself. In actuality, though, after losing the match, I did not have the desire for any of those vices. It was like someone had pulled the plug out of me.

I did have the presence of mind to know that something was wrong. This acknowledgement led me to begin reviewing some of my books from the philosophy courses I had taken while attending a local college.

The professors had instructed us in the art of self discovery and the belief system of atheism (another oxymoron). Even though I was raised under the doctrine of a monotheistic Biblical God, I began to believe their philosophical instruction. I was a god with the ability to create my own destiny.

I had fallen prey to the teachings of Friedrich Nietzsche who challenged the foundation of Christianity and traditional morality. I believed in existentialism's premise that a person's judgment is the determining factor for what is to be believed rather than religious or secular world values. Helping me conclude my thoughts was Jean-Paul Sartre's statement, "A person always has a choice, whether to comply or defy, and even a belief in God is a matter of choice."[6] Obviously, my choice to defy God was sane because there was no God.

As the months progressed, my mental anguish also revealed itself in physical ways. My 20/20 vision was now blurry. My legs had begun to atrophy. Distressingly, I also started to lose the hair on the top of my head. Even some thirty five years later, I still have daily reminders of this seven month period in my life as I have to put on my pair of eyeglasses when I wake up and carefully comb any remaining hairs over the bald spot still sporting itself on the top of my head.

After about six months, I began to have out-of-body experiences. According to recent research, these experiences can be associated with a physical or mental trauma, sensory deprivation, dehydration, sensory overload, or use of psychedelic or dissociative drugs. However, without the knowledge of these medical reasons, perceiving my physical body from a place outside of my own body had the effect of making me think I was crazy.

"Insanity equals self." I found this morsel of truth in an enlightening government report as I continued to search for answers through philosophical literature. In other words, when a person lives for himself, he will go insane. Logically, I thought, "If the ultimate act of selfishness is suicide, then I might as well try it. After all, I've been selfish. I've lived for myself and I've tried to control my own destiny. Suicide must be the only thing left."

And then, as if I was making the simple decision of whether or not I should get up off of the couch and go fix a sandwich, I reasoned, "Well, I might as well do it." Believing in my ultimate destination of suicide, I began my pursuit of the method which would end my life. Fortunately, we did not own a gun.

Maybe it was my memories of playing the game of Clue where "the colonel did it with the knife in the kitchen" because the kitchen was where I made my first suicide attempt. I pulled the butcher knife out of the drawer and I held it to my torso. However, every time I started to push it into my stomach, I chickened out. As I typed the previous line, I chuckled. Looking back, why would putting a knife into my stomach do the job when the appropriate organ to attack would have been my heart? Maybe I had heard the statement "A way to a man's heart is through his stomach" one too many times!

Back to the seriousness of my plight, I lost my nerve. "I can't do this. I can't go like this." My next attempt took me to our second story window. I raised the lower portion of our double-hung sash window and looked down to the concrete below. "If I dive head first down to the concrete, smash my head open, I'll die quickly." But just like with the butcher knife, I was too much of a coward. I could not do it. I could not jump.

Mentally searching to find an easier way, I remembered studying some eastern mysticism techniques in my philosophy courses. I could "will" my heart to stop beating. For the next few nights, I meditated with repetitive chants willing myself to die in my sleep. This attempt failed also because I always awoke to face another dreaded day.

My frustration at not being able to accomplish this "ultimate act of selfishness" was turning into anger. While I lay alone in the living room late one night staring at the ceiling, I muttered to no one in particular, "You know what? It's all God's fault."

Please remember, I considered myself an atheist. Bringing God into my religion was against what I believed. Who was I talking to? How did I transition from meditating on eastern mysticism chants to talking to a God who I had rejected years earlier?

As long as I had brought Him up, I might as well let Him know how I felt. With my fist raised toward the heavens, shaking it at God as if I had the strength to challenge Him, I defiantly scoffed, "You're not going to get me to believe in you! I don't care what you do. I'm not going to believe in you!"

As I continued chanting my refusal to believe in this God who was not supposed to exist, suddenly, on the ceiling above me, a white crackling ball of light appeared about the size of a grapefruit. It was like a sparkler. And it was sizzling .....Ssssssssszzzzzzzzzz...... I became fixated on this white light.

A ray of light suddenly entered my body and from the top of my head to the bottom of my feet, a warm energy began to flow through me. My thoughts began to race. Had God just responded to my challenge? Was this ray of light which had suddenly burst forth a direct intervention from Him? My clenched fists opened up into outstretched arms of praise and I found myself declaring "There is a God. There is a God. There ... is ... a ... God!"

Without a doubt, I had just witnessed the evidence of a supreme being. However, I did not know who this was or what it wanted. Was this the God who I had been denying? Now, instead of shaking my fist and saying, "I'm not going to believe in you," I found myself humbly petitioning God with the question, "What do you want me to do, Lord? I believe in you. I believe in you!"

This all happened past the midnight hour and I must have continued to yield my spirit in a state of wonder and bewilderment because when I finally arose from the couch, the sun was shining brightly through the living room window. For the first time in seven months, I was drawn willingly to the outdoors. I walked out of my apartment on my own accord.

Of course, if you had been driving down Bloomfield Avenue in Montclair, New Jersey, on that morning, you might have witnessed a man walking down the street talking to no one in particular and concluded he was just another drunk left over from the night before or a crazy person heading toward his bench at the park. That man would have been me. However, I was not drunk or crazy. I was perplexed and definitely off of the throne in my life.

As I wandered down the street, I verbally was seeking God's direction. "What do you want me to do? Where do you want me to go? All I've been is a pool player for the last five years. I've been in rebellion against my parents. I dropped out of school. What do you want me to do? I don't know what to do! I've got atrophy in my legs and my eyes are blurry. I've got a bald spot on my head. I wanted to commit suicide, but now all this happened. What do you want me to do with my life?"

As I spoke those last words, I stopped in my tracks as if to say, "Okay God. I'm going to stand right here until you give me direction which way to turn." Stationed there with the street on my left and the sidewalk stretched ahead, I noticed a door immediately to my right with the words "United States Navy Recruiting Office" emblazoned on the glass. I do not know what made me stop at that particular point or what drew me to the right, but as I walked through those doors, a recruiter jumped to attention and greeted me with the respect as if I was a superior officer.

Graphically, I looked anything but the part of a potential candidate for the military. My clothes were rumpled from being on the couch all night futilely attempting to kill myself. My hair was messed up except for the bald spot where there was no hair.

And we will not even talk about morning breath because I had not taken the time to brush my teeth before I ventured out into the cool October morning air.

Despite my unkempt appearance, the recruiter offered me a seat. I sat down and the recruiter started talking at a hundred miles an hour. "Son, you are just the right age. You've come to the right place. What are you going to do with your life? You don't know what you are going to do with your life? Let me tell you what the Navy can do for you."

The recruiter continued talking about this and that for the next who knows how long. My thoughts were frozen back in time and space at his recital of the exact words which I had spoken in front of his office doorway just moments before. "What do you want me to do with my life?" Could this be a coincidence or was it another direct intervention from this Spiritual Being who was so far spending His morning causing me to wonder if I really was crazy after all?

The year was now 1976. The United States had discontinued the draft in 1973 so that there was no more mandatory conscription. Our country's defense was now made up of an all-volunteer military force.

I had "dodged the bullet" and avoided Vietnam six years earlier when the lottery was instituted. Rather than serve my country, I had chosen to do nothing but drugs, alcohol, women, gambling, playing pool, and essentially destroying my life. The recruiter was now offering, "Son, we can help you!" He did not know my life story.

Looking for an escape from this bombardment of information, I excused myself and went into the bathroom. With the door locked, I looked at my reflection in the mirror as if I needed an eyewitness to what I was about ready to say.

"Okay God. You got me into this. You appeared to me last night in a light on the ceiling. What do you want me to do? I'm too weak to enter the Navy. I'm atrophied."

As if to prove my point, I got down on the floor (which upheld the military standard of latrine cleanliness) and I started doing pushups right there in the bathroom. Suddenly my body was experiencing newfound strength and I found myself miraculously doing about fifteen pushups. Without even a hint of exhaustion, I murmured, "Wow. I haven't done pushups or any kind of exercise for seven months!"

I stood back up and rejoined my comrade in the mirror. "Okay God, are you telling me to join? I can't make this decision on my own." Then, out of nowhere, the following words tumbled out of my mouth, "Do you want me to call my father, God?"

My father. Calmness swelled over me as I thought of this man who I had treated like the enemy for so many years. This man who had played catch with me as a boy and who had installed a pool table in our basement because he knew I loved billiards. My heart filled with an emotional pool of memories. The last time I had seen him was at the $5000 match which had triggered my seven month depression. Even after learning he had been injured in a car crash a few months later, I was too downcast to even call to see how he was. I would call now!

With newfound focus, I marched out of the bathroom and announced to the recruiter, "My dad was a World War II hero and he fought twelve naval battles in the war. I am going to call him and get his advice and I'll get back to you tomorrow."

Back in my apartment I picked up the phone and called home. My dad answered.

"Dad, it's Stephen."

"Yes Son, what do you need?"

"Dad, I'm thinking about joining the Navy."

"You are?"

"I want to know what you think, Dad."

"Well Son, you obviously want to talk about this. I'll get in my car right now and I'll be there in about two and a half hours."

I was waiting on the steps of the apartment building when he arrived. Following him to the parking lot, I got in the passenger seat where we sat and talked for the next couple of hours. No hugs. No tears. Just a man to man conversation between a father who knew that his son had to find his own way and a son who was finally allowing someone to help him find it.

"Dad, I messed my life up for the last six years."

"I understand, Son."

"Dad, this is a chance to do something with my life."

42

"Yes, it is a chance, Son."

"Dad, you were in the Navy. You've always told me good things about the Navy. Would the Navy be a good choice?"

"Yes, the Navy would be a good choice."

My dad never tried to persuade. He listened and affirmed and then he drove away.

The next day I went down to the United States Navy recruiting office.

"Sir, I'm here to sign up for the United States Navy."

"A decision you will not regret. I've got your contracts right here for you to sign. Tomorrow, be at the Newark train station at 10:00 o'clock. We will be sending you to boot camp in Orlando, Florida."

That quick. My life was changed in the time it took for me to sign my name. I had not even told my wife yet! In my usual autonomous fashion, I went home and shared with her, after the fact, what I was going to do.

"Patti, I just joined the United States Navy about an hour ago."

She turned and studied me for a moment and then she contemplatively said, "Okay. That sounds like a good move."

Patti would always give me an encouraging response. No matter what I chose to do with my life, she would offer her supportive assurances. We sat and talked for awhile until she asked the question which brought a silent thoughtfulness to the both of us.

"When do you have to leave?"

"I have to be at the train station tomorrow to go down to Orlando."

"So soon? Just remember I'll be here when you come back."

CHAPTER 6

"Pride goes before destruction,
and haughtiness before a fall."
(Proverbs 16:18)

The train ride from Newark to Orlando lasted over twenty hours. During such an interval, a person has a lot of time to reflect. And I did.

While sitting in coach staring at the back of the seat in front of me, I was beginning to get a little nervous. The reality of what I had done less than twenty-four hours before was beginning to sink in. Steve Lillis had joined the United States Navy. Since God had directed me to make this decision, I began silently talking to Him.

"Well God, I'm here on this train because of you. You're the one who appeared to me in that light. I know you are real and joining the Navy is where you want me to be so I'm counting on your help."

I quickly discovered my need for His help. Upon arriving in Orlando, military personnel were standing on the dock waiting as if incoming prisoners were arriving. What did I get myself into? Within minutes, I was corralled into a group of other new recruits and a man began to bark, **"I am your senior drill instructor. From now on you will speak only when spoken to and the first and last words out of your filthy traps will be "sir." Do you understand?"**

Only some within my group seemed to grasp the simplicity of this basic command because only a few answered "Sir, yes sir!" Our lack of audible rejoinder only aggravated the drill instructor further.

"I can't hearrrrrrrrrrr you! Do you understand?"

"SIR, YES SIR" (Now we sounded like the Vienna Boys Choir).

Our new alpha dog continued, **"If you inferior mongrels happen to survive recruit training, you will amount to someone worth representing our great country. But until that day, you are nothing. You are the scum of the earth. Because I am heartless, you will not like me. I don't care. The more you hate me the more you will learn. I am hard, but I am fair. You are all equally worthless. Right now you are just a bunch of mangy looking dogs, but when I get done with you, you'll be able to look at yourself in the mirror. Do you inept cast-offs understand?**

"SIR, YES SIR!"

Being spoken to in such acrimonious tones was new to my life experience. Of course, the next three and a half months of grueling boot camp taught me to withstand such verbal abuse (not to mention physical challenge). However, God had directed my path into the military and this belief gave me the courage and strength to persevere.

The Navy was being good to me. I received my first pair of prescription glasses which allowed me to see without the blurriness. I got my head shaved, of course, which hid the memory of my bald spot for the time being. In addition, the atrophy in my legs began to dissipate most likely due to the regimented exercise.

After boot camp graduation, I was assigned to my first ship, the U.S.S. Austin dry docked in Baltimore, Maryland. Receiving a three day leave before I was required to report for duty, I went home to see Patti. She undoubtedly was encouraged to see the Navy's positive influence in my life.

Upon reporting back for duty, my first assignment was to chip paint off of the hull of our ship. Because I had signed up for regular Navy and did not sign up for a school in the Navy, my assignments were manual labor oriented. Despite the mundane work assignment, I continued my conversations with God. "Well, God, I guess this is what you had for me. Chipping paint is what you must want me to do."

Up until this point in my military career, I had basically kept to myself. About the fourth week after reporting for duty in Baltimore, some of my shipmates invited me to join them one evening for a night on the town. I knew of their escapades on liberty because I had overheard the stories upon their return from carousing on previous outings. Drinking. Drugs. Women. Pool.

I had not played pool since my loss of the $5000 match which resulted in my spiraling depression and I had not been involved with the drinking, drugs, and women scene since then as well. I found myself being interested in joining these guys. Not for the drinking, drugs, and women part, but for the opportunity to play some pool. At the time, my intentions seemed harmless enough.

We arrived at the bar and everything was going great until I was challenged to a game of pool. As the balls started to drop into the pockets, the jaws of my shipmates also began to drop in disbelief at my ability to play. Immediately they started to devise schemes.

"Boy, can we make money with you!"

"Oh no. No!" I countered. "Leave me out. I don't gamble. I'm not going to get involved with hustling again."

Unfettered by my opposition, they continued. "Wait until the Captain hears about you. He's going to want to know about this."

"Listen guys. I'm here to have fun. Let's just play some pool."

However, the Captain did hear about it and on the next day I was called into his office. He ordered me to sit down.

"Lillis. Is it true what I've heard about you? Your shipmates are saying that you are the best pool player they have ever seen around these parts. How good do you really play?"

"Well sir, I was actually one of the top players in the world before I joined the service. I was on the pro tour and in the past year I had some top ten finishes. I was one of the rising stars among the professionals, but I gave it all up to be in the Navy."

My last line was indeed a stretch of the imagination when it came to the truth of why I had joined. I had given up a miserable life of depression to be in the Navy and God had been a big influence in my decision. Nevertheless, I chose to deny God's presence in my life and, instead, I made it sound like I had made this great sacrificial decision all on my own.

As I sat in front of this man who held position and power over me, my self confidence and self image reemerged with a new vitality. I perceived my pecking order placement was advancing due to my pool playing prowess. The old Steve Lillis was quickly resurfacing.

Scenes from my youth were about to repeat themselves. After moving to Wayne as a teenager, I had been despised by my peers because of my athletic talents and the favoritism awarded to me by the coaches. Here in the Navy, I was going to be despised by my shipmates because of my pool playing talent and the special treatment granted to me by my superior officer.

Please understand, I was not rejected by my high school peers because of my athleticism. I was shunned by others because of my boastful pride. My success was always about Steve Lillis. Encouraging others to succeed was not a part of my playbook. Even though I had chosen to follow Bobby Richardson as a role model when I was a kid, I failed to see what made him great. Bobby had a servant's heart toward his teammates. He inspired players both on and off the field. He willingly helped others and he was humble. On the contrary, my goal was to be the best at what I did and leave everyone else in the dust behind me. I failed to learn the important lessons of kindness, love, and humility.

Upon the Captain's learning of my professional ranking, he responded to my erroneous statement about giving up pool so that I could join the Navy. "Not so fast, Lillis. Maybe you don't have to give up pool. I'm going to make you a deal. How would you like to go to the world championships with the United States Navy backing you? And I'm going to send you with a Navy photographer and a Navy journalist. We are going to have posters with your picture on it and we are going to get you into newspaper and magazine print. You are going to be famous. When people see your name and photo, they are going to think 'Navy.' All you have to do is bring me a letter substantiating your professional standing and I'll make you a star. Can you bring me proof Lillis?"

"Yes, sir. The president of the professional pool player's association is a good friend of mine. He can supply the letter." I was speaking of Ray Martin, BCA Hall of Famer.

"Is it a deal then, Lillis?"

"Yes, sir. It sure beats chipping paint, sir."

"Lillis, when I get that letter, you will not be chipping paint any more. You are going to take care of your hands. You are not going to have any hard duty and you are going to do a lot of pool playing. Sound good, Lillis?"

"Sir, yes sir!"

We struck a deal in his office. The letter came and I was exempted from all hard duty. Of course my shipmates were not as enthusiastic about this new arrangement as I was. The majority were righteously indignant. Many on my ship bore scars from Vietnam and were not star struck with this pool playing prodigy who was being treated like a prissy. The scale of justice was tilted unfairly in their minds. Just because I could play pool did not make me better than regular Navy. Who did I think I was? The ranks were divided. Them against me.

Within a few months, I was sent off to a World 14.1 Straight Pool Championship where I competed against the "Who's Who In Pool." I took 9th place. Hall of Famer Luther Lassiter finished one place above me and Hall of Famer Pat Fleming finished one place behind me.

True to the plan, the press did report on my being the first player to compete in world pool championships sponsored by the United States Navy. I was successfully fulfilling the role of "poster boy" in order to help recruit other young men into the Navy. My Captain was ecstatic upon my return and eager to learn the date of the next event.

Others on the ship were not so pleased. The Chief Petty Officer, my immediate superior, was already angry because I had been pulled from regular duty and he became even more infuriated upon learning that my expenses had been paid for by the ship's services money. He confronted me on deck one day and with indignation in his tone said, "They are using our ship's money for you to go play pool and you are not even doing any hard labor! I don't agree with that and furthermore I'm going to find a way to stop you."

His threat went in one ear and out of the other because my ego had been stoked back to life when the Captain had endorsed my talents and sanctioned my tournament duties. With my arrogance now fully flared, I heatedly retorted, "You can't stop me. Furthermore, if you have a problem with my playing pool, you can go see the Captain because I'm untouchable. So get out of my face!"

Upon hearing my defiance, the Chief Petty Officer threw me up against the bulkhead of the ship. With my neck in the grasp of his hand, he growled, "I will find a way to stop you."

Challenging his threat, I replied, "You know something? You're going to have to kill me. And if you are not ready to kill me right here and right now, then you better get your hands off of me!"

He released his hold and walked away. However, his opportunity for revenge was only a few short months away.

The Captain soon sent me to my second event which was the 1977 World 9-Ball Championship. Coincidentally, this tournament was held in Baltimore, Maryland, where my ship was dry docked. As before, journalists were among the attendees, but this time they would get the real scoop about Steve Lillis.

Once again I placed within the top ten coming in 9th, but this time I had defeated Allen Hopkins who was the newly crowned World Open 14.1 Straight Pool Champion. Allen was the second youngest player in the history of pocket billiard tournament competition to win this prestigious title. A few of his other titles included the 1977 U.S. Open 9-Ball Champion and PPPA World 9-Ball Champion as well as the future honor of being inducted into the Billiard Congress of America Hall of Fame in 2008.[8] Obviously, he was the favored player to win.

My unexpected victory over Allen created media interest. A press conference ensued and I was asked the following question by one of the reporters. "Well, Steve, now that you are representing the United States Navy as a professional pool player, what do you see as your future with the Navy?"

There it was, the perfect "poster boy" opportunity to respond. Of course, I had been primed beforehand with an abundance of many recruiting dialogues which would have brought honor to the Navy. For example, I could have responded with:

> "My Navy experience has already shaped my future through unparalleled career potential as well as providing me with a lifestyle of freedom and personal growth which I had been seeking before joining this great organization. Whether I am using my pool skills or the many other skills that the Navy is currently equipping me with, I look

forward to a future of serving my country in whatever capacity I am needed."

Or another option might have been:

"Our country's Navy is a force as relevant today as it has been historically significant. The times may change and the threats may become more obscure, but now more than ever, the Navy is something to be aware of. Something to be thankful for. Something to be proud of. And with all of my skills, whether they be on or off of the pool table, I look forward to a future of serving our country alongside others who are strong in character and strong in might."[7]

With these great responses filed in my mental library, I instead chose to go off script. Can I blame anyone but myself? No. My responsibility rests solely on my sin of self serving pride.

Admittedly, I had been feeling like an outcast. My cavalier attitude was not conducive to building friendships or even civil relationships with either my shipmates or my superior officer. I was not really looking forward to a long stint in the Navy as a loner. My sights were increasingly becoming focused on getting back out into the real world of pool and mixing with the crowd who I was comfortable with. Stupidly, I shared this life vision with the press and made it appear like I was interested only in my own pursuits, thereby making my service in the Navy only a means to an end.

When the reporter asked the question, "Well Steve, now that you are representing the United States Navy as a professional pool player, what do you see as your future with the Navy?" I responded:

"The Navy is a great organization to have as my sponsor right now. As far as my future? When my time is served, I will continue to pursue my career in professional pool."

50

My answer not only sounded like I was taking advantage of the Navy, but that the Navy was holding me as a prisoner until the day of my release. Needless to say, this negative publicity did not sit well with my Captain. He had been my only lifeline in the midst of the waves of anger spewed at me from my grudging shipmates and immediate supervisor. My protected status was about to change.

Upon my return to the ship, the Chief Petty Officer said to me with a nasty gleam in his eye, "The Captain wants to see you immediately in his office. After he is done with you, report *IMMEDIATELY* back to me for your new duty roster."

Up until then, I had not really valued the privileges which I had been granted. We have all heard the expression "We don't really appreciate what we have until we lose it." This was one of those "life lesson" experiences for me, and I knew that I had lost it.

The Captain scowled at me as I was ushered into his office. "Lillis. No more pool tournaments. You're done. I read the interview from the last tournament and your responses are *NOT* the kind of print I wanted to see. The Navy is no longer going to *'SERVE'* as your sponsor. Instead, you are going to *'SERVE'* the Navy. I don't know who you think you are, but from now on, you are going to be ranked lower than the barnacles you will be scraping off of this ship. I am turning you over to your immediate superior and I wash my hands of you. If people used to think of you as a 'captain's boy,' I have made it clear to everyone that your special duty assignment has been revoked. You are on your own from now on. Don't even come near me. DISMISSED!"

Dismissed. I would have rather been sent to the brig and faced a court martial. News travels quickly on a ship and my mind could envision the lynch mob already beginning to assemble and, trust me, there was plenty of rope on this Navy vessel for them to accomplish their task. Fortunately, my "hanging" theory proved to be wrong. Instead, drowning was going to be the preferred method of choice.

When I reported back to the Chief Petty Officer, he was anticipating my return like a shark circling his prey. The first words out of his mouth were, "You're dead. When this ship gets under way, we are going to enjoy watching you over the side with your head bobbing up and down in the water as you're drowning."

"Really?" I retorted back in anger. "You know what? You better kill me right now because I'll kill you first."

The Chief Petty Officer, seeing my response was now merely an idle threat, just laughed and said, "Ha! We got you now." Then, with complete satisfaction of his regained power, he assigned me to hard duty. On the next day, I found myself hanging over the side of the ship chipping paint while suspended about one hundred feet over the concrete pavement below.

The process of chipping paint requires the use of a power grinder which efficiently sands the paint off of the hull. Those who become faint at the sight of blood might want to avoid the mental images of what can happen when the spinning saw-like disc on this tool comes into contact with the operator's hand. A bloody mess and serious injury ensues.

On my second day of hard duty, while I was hanging precariously over the side of the ship, the safety belt which held my dangerous power grinder snapped in two. The man-eating tool swung over and sliced directly into my left hand causing spurts of blood to spit out in all directions.

Even before my first yell for help, my thoughts raced to whether I would be able to play pool again because the blade had sliced the hand I used to bridge my cue. Apparently, mine were not the only thoughts focused on my ability to play pool. Word had traveled fast about my injury. By the time I was pulled up to the deck, a reception committee of crew members was already gathered to greet me. Mockingly they sneered, "Now let's see you play pool!"

With my right hand still in perfect operating condition, I grabbed a tool leaning against the railing and began angrily wielding it at my avengers. Chasing after anyone within my swinging distance, my goal was to hurt someone. After the deck was cleared of my taunting shipmates, I went to the dispensary where word of my injury had already traveled to the medic. When I walked in and said, "Fix my hand." He responded, "Here's a band-aid. Fix it yourself."

They were all against me. They all wanted me out. With blood dripping out of my sliced hand, I reasoned, "If *out* is where they want me, then *out* is where I will go. I ran off of the ship. I went UA. Unauthorized Absence.

Escaping to the only place where I had felt accepted, I ran to the local billiard room where my pool playing buddies hung out. Needless to say, when they saw me walk in cradling my hand in the folds of my red stained shirt, I became the focus of their attention.

"What happened to your hand, Steve? Are you still going to be able to play pool?"

Obviously, they understood my love for the sport. In unbelief and horror, my friends listened to the story. Just for the record, *my hand hurt*!

One of the guys was a lawyer who knew the legal ramifications of my being UA. He strongly advised me to go back and turn myself in. However, he was not arbitrarily sending me back. He had a plan, a legal plan.

My attorney friend had learned an advantageous fact about my enlistment through our past conversations. I had been randomly selected to be a participant in a pilot program when I joined. Recruits under this program were allowed to opt out of the Navy without consequence anytime within the first six months of service. After the first six months had expired, a recruit was allowed to be honorably discharged within the next six months only upon the signed approval of the Captain. At the completion of one year, a recruit was required to fulfill the entire military contract term.

I was only in my eleventh month of service which was a material fact capable of tilting the scales in my favor. After listening to the counsel of my attorney, I confidently returned to the ship and turned myself in.

With my hand still oozing blood through the scabs attempting to form, I took immediate control of the situation and demanded, "I want to see the Captain right away. My attorney is waiting for my phone call confirming that proper medical attention has been given to my injury. If I don't see the Captain right away, you're not going to like the headlines in the morning paper tomorrow."

Within the hour, I was escorted into the Captain's office where I was greeted by a man who knew that I now had the upper hand, even though it was an injured hand!

"Have a seat, Lillis. What can I do for you today?"

"Sir, I am electing to be discharged from the Navy per my recruiting contract and I want your required signature on the necessary documents without delay. I also want my hand fixed and I want it fixed *NOW*."

"Consider it done."

I was transported to the naval hospital where the doctors stitched up my hand and within twenty four hours I was on a train headed home with my discharge papers signed by the Captain.

CHAPTER 7

"For the Lord sees clearly what a man does,
examining every path he takes."
(Proverbs 5:21)

If I had been depressed before entering the Navy due to my feelings of failure and being forsaken by friends and family, then you can imagine my mental state after this stint among sailors who successfully seasoned my life with stressful suffering. I was an emotional wreck. The whole saga of my military pool playing career had left me walking a psychological tightrope on which I was about to lose my balance.

Of course, my wife, Patti, was home waiting for me, ready and hopeful to resume our marriage, but I was not. Home was not going to be where I found solace. The local tavern would provide relief from my personal pity party and I lost no time in immersing myself once again into this environment offering escape. Within hours of my arrival home, I was sitting at the bar. Drunk.

Over the next few weeks my relationships with friends were renewed. As I revisited my old haunts, I was welcomed back as a local hero, "Hey everybody! Steve's here! We've been reading about your pool playing. Come on over and have a drink. We've missed you!"

This ticker tape reception from pool players excited about my achievements soon had me contemplating the words which had cost me my Navy career:

> As far as my future, when my time is served, I will
> continue to pursue my career in professional pool.

A new vision for my life began to unfold because *today* was my future, my time was served and I was now free to pursue my career in pool. Sharing my dream with Patti one night, I asked her to join me in the quest of my professional career.

"Patti, run away with me. Come and travel the country with me."

"No, Steve. I don't want to go on the road. I'd have to quit my job."

"But Patti, we can take all of my newfound fame and go around the country earning money playing pool."

"No. You go by yourself. I'll be here when you get back."

Those words were not what I wanted to hear. In fact, Patti had rarely denied me before. She had always gone along with whatever I wanted. I was getting tired of her patronizing attitude of "I'll be here for you, Steve. I'll be here for you, Steve." Well, she was not there for me. She was off in her own world. She was into her work and whatever else kept her busy.

Like a spoiled child I went back to my friends at the bars and pool halls. Dejected, I began to spiral downhill even faster. I was back to doing drugs with my crowd of cronies.

One day while lingering in one of the pool playing bars with my buddies, a new young woman entered the scene and I immediately noticed her pool playing ability (not to mention her attractiveness!). Since I was always up for a game of pool, I made myself available for a challenge match with this girl whose name I soon learned was Camille.

Have you ever met someone and immediately felt a bond develop? That was the way I felt with Camille. We hit it off right then and there. I fell in love with her. I do not know if I fell in love with a romantic image or a person who was struggling to pull herself up from the bottom dregs of life like I was, but there was something irresistible about her.

Our relationship quickly advanced from playing pool together, to sharing drugs, and then to sharing sex together. Yes, I was unfaithful and yet I am not going to make excuses for my infidelity. I was not attending church. I definitely was not serving God anymore or even thinking about Him. Even with my "light on the ceiling" vision, I no longer acknowledged God's presence in my life. My interests were focused on pool, drugs, and now Camille.

Still desiring to cash in on my pool playing fame, I shared my dream with Camille of wanting to go on the road and play in tournaments across the country. Unlike Patti, she was eager to join me as I pursued my ambition. Her interest sparked my determination to chase my dream. The U.S. 9-Ball Open Championships in Norfolk, Virginia, were less than a month away. I made the decision to enter the competition which effectively re-energized my pool playing career.

The day quickly arrived for me to leave. Not having my own car, I hitched a ride with a couple of pool playing friends, one of which was Allen Hopkins (the same Allen who had triggered my final catastrophic media interview which effectively ended my military service). As we departed from New Jersey to Virginia via highway US-13, our conversations ranged from talking shop to sparring about which one of us was going to become the new U.S. 9-Ball Open Champion. However, underneath the mask of my self-confident exterior resided a dismal, dejected, depressed, and downcast man. The recent introduction of mass drugs into my system after almost two years of being clean was taking their toll on my body, especially my pool playing body. My game was suffering.

Much the same as adrenaline can help someone compensate for weakness in a demanding situation, my cocky attitude could counterbalance my game deficiencies. Such was the case at the U.S. 9-Ball Open Championships. Despite my drug riddled body, I had advanced to the money match and I was playing professional pool player Jimmy Mataya, nicknamed "Pretty Boy Floyd." Jimmy was on his way to becoming a world champion with over thirty major titles. A few years after this event, in 1982, he married Ewa Svensson, 17, of Sweden (who was later inducted into the Billiard Congress of America Hall of Fame as Ewa Mataya Laurance in 2004). Although they later divorced, their marriage at the time was effectively recognized as pool's first "power couple."[9]

During Jimmy's and my matchup, I was the one wielding the "power." The scoreboard showed "Lillis" ahead by a long shot and "Mataya" trailing. However, my arrogance, which was fueling my body to perform, had also provoked the audience to despise me. Steve Lillis was not the favored player to win.

The competitive environment in pool is similar to the sport of tennis because viewers are to remain silent during play. Only after the execution of a shot or the completion of a game should the spectators show their support and enthusiasm through applause. As I pretentiously ran the table game after game against Jimmy, the audience remained condemningly silent thereby expressing their contempt for me.

I probably would have ruined the crowd's day had I continued on to win, but something inexplicable happened to me which had never happened before. Suddenly, my right arm locked up in the middle of a game. Literally, my arm was paralyzed. I could not shoot anymore. I was crippled.

The audience perceived that something was wrong. I was powerless to pocket a ball. New life breathed through the onlookers as they not only hoped for my opponent's triumph, but also for his chance to deliver my defeat to them on a silver platter. After every shot Jimmy made, no matter how simple or complex, the crowd spurred him on with enthusiastic applause and shouts of affirmation. With me now helplessly stunned by my inability to confidently hold my cue stick, Jimmy offensively ran the table to the tune of eight games in a row thereby taking me out of the tournament. I still ponder whether the standing ovation at the end was more for Jimmy winning or for my losing. Probably both.

By now the reader should know me well enough to conjecture my reaction to this abasing loss. My last defeat at the $5000 match in front of my family threw me into the depths of despair for seven months, culminating in thoughts of suicide. Mentally, I was already on the fast track to the same psychological destination and I was not even out of the front door yet!

With my cue packed away in its case and my purpose for coming to the U.S. Open now just a pitiful pilgrimage, I walked out of the tournament building's front door ready to end it all when who did I meet walking into the building at the same exact moment as I was walking out? Camille! Upon seeing her, I asked, "What are you doing here? I just lost."

My question was really a pointless one because I did not really care why Camille was there. I was just glad to see her. In addition, my immediate confession of failure to someone who loved me was acting like a healing balm over my wounded ego and pride. My spirit lifted. I was curiously distracted by the reason which brought this lovely angel to stand in front of me some three hundred miles from where I had last seen her.

Camille responded, "I wanted to come see you so I got in the car and drove down. What happened? Who did you lose to?"

"Jimmy Mataya, but I don't really want to talk about it. I'm heading out. Do you want to come with me?"

"Sure."

Camille turned and led the way to her car. As we walked, my thoughts of defeat were distracted by this beautiful decoy who destiny had delivered to my doorstep. We got in the car and began to drive. At some point I must have asked if we should head home because I remember Camille said "No."

The context of that simple word seemed to open the escape hatch through which my life could start anew because "home" was not where I wanted to go either. Instead, our journey led us south to Florida where we stayed with one of my old high school drug buddies. Even though we easily fit in, we were beginning to experience the futility of the drug scene lifestyle. These feelings soon led to our joint decision to quit drugs. As our alternative, we chose to pursue the path of professional pool. Camille and I became road players as well as partners.

Our escape from home had initially driven us south, but we would soon be driving north, east, and west because Camille and I spent the next three years traveling on the pool playing circuit. We drove 85,000 miles stopping at every pool room and playing in every tournament we found along the way.

I was literally on the road to achieving my dream of becoming the pool champion of the world. As I consistently placed in the money rounds in tournament after tournament, my name and reputation was beginning to build up across the country.

CHAPTER 8

"Listen as wisdom calls out!
Hear as understanding raises her voice!"
(Proverbs 8:1)

Another man's name and reputation was also building up within the billiard industry. I had first crossed paths with this man back in 1976 before I lost the $5000 match in front of my family. The month was February and I had flown down from New Jersey to Baton Rouge, Louisiana, to compete in a professional tournament. During my practice warm ups, I noticed a guy performing trick shots over on another pool table.

"Who's the big guy over there?" I asked a man sitting on a bar stool nearby.

"Oh, that's Mike Massey. Watch some of his shots. Incredible. They gave him a free entry if he would just entertain us with some trick shots."

From my perspective, this "Mike guy" was earning his free entry because he had evoked a *cause for pause* moment in my day. I walked over and joined the rest of the crowd who was watching this trick shot artist. Suddenly, as if he was taking his cue from the onlookers who had gathered around him, Mike laid down his cue stick on the pool table and said, "Let me tell you about Jesus."

I turned to a man standing next to me and mocked, "Did he just say what I think he said?"

"Yep! Keep listening. It gets worse. He goes into this preach job every so often once he sees a new crowd of unsuspecting spectators gathered around."

As my ears turned to listen and my heart turned away in rejection, Mike continued his sermon, "Yes, Jesus has changed my life. I used to do drugs and alcohol and now I'm married and have two kids and I'm back playing pool again. But now I'm playing pool for Jesus!" Blah, blah, blah.

With my ears and heart now at odds with one another, my mouth decided to put in its two cents. "You've gotta be kidding. Is this guy out of his mind or what? The only time I ever hear Jesus mentioned in the pool room is as a curse word."

The sincerity of Mike Massey's words must have made an impact on me because not only did I remember him, but if I was to be honest, my heart was tempted to be swayed by what my ears had heard. My mouth decided to just remain silent on the subject until I crossed paths again with Mike while Camille and I were on our road tour.

A tournament had drawn us to North Carolina. While waiting for the event to start, I saw Mike over at a table practicing and I decided to walk over and introduce myself.

"Hi, Mike. How are you doing?"

Surprisingly, Mike responded, "Oh yeah, I remember you. How are you doing Steve?"

Mike's recognition of me served as proof of my reputation building up among the players because, trust me, I had not gone up and introduced myself to this Jesus freak back when I first saw him in Baton Rouge. However, the seed which he planted back then must have chosen that precise moment to sprout because, in an attempt to make myself look like I was in agreement with Mike's beliefs, I offered my own life changing testimony.

"I want you to know Mike, I have stopped doing drugs and I have stopped doing alcohol. And you know something? I remember what you said about Jesus and I'm on the right track."

Admittedly, I was not entirely on the right track, but I thought I was on the right track. After all, Camille and I did make a commitment to stop using drugs and alcohol prior to our decision to begin our pool playing journey. We even turned on the television in the hotel room and listened to the televangelists periodically. Of course we were not going to church, but we talked about God. In a sense, we were informally seeking God. We felt like God was on our side now because we no longer were doing drugs and alcohol. Taking advantage of the opportunity, I wanted to boast, "Hey Mike. I've cleaned up my act, too." I was proud to say those words.

Camille also had a moment of declaring her position with God at another North Carolina tournament. Looking back at these memories, I realize now that people are at different stages on their journey with God and yet He is faithful to meet them where they are at. After all, why would God want to have anything to do with Camille and me? I was separated from my wife, yet I lived with Camille and we traveled around the country as if we were converted souls just because we had cleaned up our act and no longer took drugs.

We were also trying to play pool the right way. Please remember, I knew how to play pool the wrong way from my hustling days. However, life was now on the "up and up." I gave pool lessons and Camille helped me to promote and organize tournaments.

In fact, we promoted the first professional women's tournament held in North Carolina. The year was 1979. LoreeJon Oganowski (later known as LoreeJon Jones) competed in this first time event. She was a young player from New Jersey who two years earlier, at age 11, had achieved pro player status with the Women's Professional Billiard Association. She was known as "Queen of the Hill" and two years later at age 15, LoreeJon won the World Straight Pool Tournament becoming the youngest player, male or female, ever to win a world title. This is a feat noted by the Guinness Book of World Records. At the time of her 2002 induction into the Billiard Congress of America Hall of Fame, LoreeJon held more than 50 titles and was recognized five times as "Player of the Year" by Pool & Billiards Magazine and Billiards Digest.[10]

Returning to my story about Camille, I still simultaneously cringe and smile when I remember the scene of her shouting words at Mark, the owner of the pool room where we were directing a tournament. Mark and his wife were our good friends and they would invite us to stay in their home whenever we passed through their area. However, our friendship was probably founded more on the business side of our relationship versus the personal side. We had promoted many professional pool tournaments at his business establishment thereby drawing in the patronage of many professional and local top players. We had also organized the first North Carolina professional women's tournament at Mark's venue. Interestingly, years later, North Carolina became the center of women's professional pool.

The personal side of our friendship held the irony of Camille's little outburst. Mark and his wife did not believe in God or Christianity. They were atheists.

With the stage now set, I was playing in the men's side and Camille was playing in the women's side. Camille got knocked out of the tournament early by LoreeJon, but I had advanced to the top four in the men's bracket. I was motivated to win because a significant amount of prize money had been added to the pot and winning was how I now earned my living.

Camille was basically running the tournament because I was still playing matches. Mark inexplicably began to not only make it difficult for Camille to do her job, but also began to create sufficient interruptions and distractions in my game. He was obviously attempting to shark me into a loss. I will never know the reason Mark turned on us and yet I will always remember Camille's reaction to his opposition.

The tension had taken them into the back room behind closed doors. Suddenly, in the silence of my semi final match of the tournament, I, along with everyone else in the room, heard an argument ensuing between the two of them. Talk about a "Wanna Get Away?" moment from those Southwest Airlines commercials. I wanted a plane ticket to anywhere right about then because the content of the words flying through the air was Camille's chewing out Mark for all of the sabotage he was doing in an effort to get me to lose.

The ears on every head in the room were tuned into the broadcast bellowing out from behind that closed door while the eyes on every one of those same heads were zeroing in on me. Then, right before we heard the door slam and saw Camille exiting the back room, I heard Camille yell out at the top of her lungs these final words to our atheist friend,

"You will not stop us because we've got God on our side."

As I look back, we really believed her declaration. Camille and I really believed God was on our side because we were trying to promote Mark's pool tournament the right way. We had managed it to the letter of the "pool law" by being fair, being upfront, being honest, being decent, and being courteous.

Even today, over thirty years later, the memory of this episode reminds me to be patient with others who I perceive as being hypocrites because, not only was I also a hypocrite, I still am one today in some areas of my life. As I continue to meet people who are making wrong life choices, I look back at my own life and think, "They are at a particular stage in their journey. How can I judge them? How can I legalistically say, 'You're wrong, wrong, wrong. You've got this sin, this sin, and this sin,' when God graciously accepted me for where I was at?" (With that said, I would like to apologize in advance for an upcoming scene where I despised a man because I perceived him as a hypocrite. When we get there, please forgive my obvious failure to apply the life lesson of acceptance and patience with others.)

Even though Camille and I were not living according to God's good and perfect will, God took us "as is." He accepted us for who we were and allowed us to grow at our own pace into more obedience to His Word. In fact, without me even realizing what I was doing, God used me in another professional pool tournament to lead someone to follow Him.

This time we were in Colorado Springs. I had finished fourth place in a national tournament against some of the best players in the world. After the tournament, a guy by the name of Jeff Ballantyne came up to me with a question. Through our introductory conversation, I deduced that Jeff was a broken down road player. He had traveled all over the country, even as far as Alaska, playing pool, gambling, and doing drugs. He now stood in front of me seeking advice.

"Steve, I'm really impressed with the way you play and I've heard about your exploits traveling the country. Can you give me some names and information so that I can go make some money?"

I recognized myself in this player and since I did not really like whom I had been, I did not want to help him become who he thought he wanted to be. If he wanted a name, I was going to give him a name. With complete unawareness, I did exactly what God simply asks any of us to do. I responded, "Jeff, I'll give you something better. I'll give you Jesus. You see, it's all meaningless apart from knowing the truth about God."

I began to talk with Jeff about God as I knew God and then we parted ways. Two months later, Jeff called me. He had given his heart to the Lord. He said, "Steve, I want you to know our conversation in Colorado Springs led me to the Lord and I've quit pool. I am going to enroll in Bible school. Thank you!"

Having no clue what I had done and not fully understanding what he meant about being "led to the Lord," I just responded with, "That's great news Jeff! God bless you in your decision." After his phone call I sat scratching my head with a sense of bewilderment. All I had done was tell Jeff about Jesus and how if we want to live right in His eyes, we have to quit drinking and doing drugs like Camille and I had done. I never said, or even implied, that he had to quit pool and go to Bible school.

Jeff did go on to Bible school and he did quit pool temporarily for quite a few years. In fact, God must have orchestrated this interlude between Jeff and me because Jeff will eventually serve as a board member for a Gospel trick shot ministry which I will start years later. Our love for the sport of pool will blend together with our love for God. Jeff is my very good friend and, as of the writing of this book, currently serves the Lord at the University of Minnesota as a campus pastor of International Student Friendship Ministries.

CHAPTER 9

"Disregarding another person's faults preserves love;
telling about them separates close friends."
(Proverbs 17:9)

During our three year traveling odyssey, Camille and I lived a gypsy lifestyle. From 1978 through 1980, we experienced an 85,000 mile road trip during an era of time revisited now only through memories and old photos. Never again will we see gas prices averaging $1.00 per gallon and motel rates averaging $50 to $75 *per week*. Living on the road was simple and affordable back then, unless, of course, you totaled the car.

When Camille and I left Florida after we made the decision to quit drugs, we eventually headed west to Phoenix, Arizona where I was in a car accident. Another car came at me while I was in an intersection and Camille's car, given to her by family, was beyond repair. Using the insurance money, we purchased a 1973 Pontiac Catalina with about 30,000 original miles on it.

Camille managed our finances very frugally and kept a log of every penny spent on gas, hotels, and food during those three years. Pancake mix was our staple. We prepared pancakes on our little electric griddle practically every day for breakfast and even many of our dinners. Because the microwave was still a relatively new invention, we also owned a one burner appliance. Eventually we graduated to a two burner, which was a big upgrade for us at the time. Boiling water provided the foundation to many a warm meal. We also hauled around our refrigerator - an ice chest. We bought a lot of ice!

All of our kitchenette equipment, accumulated personal belongings, billiard accessories, and the clothes on our back traveled in the Pontiac with us. To her credit, Camille knew how to pack! Those weighty cars were designed with a large trunk and Camille had every little nook and cranny covered. She could get all of our worldly possessions into the trunk and interior of that car. The back seat was not only packed to the brim, but architected to provide a little traveling perch. As we crisscrossed the country in our Catalina, Camille would casually crawl into her comfy car couch and take catnaps.

Of course we took turns driving. In order to maximize gas mileage, fifty miles an hour was our average speed. Those muscle cars were major gas guzzlers. The country was beginning to respond to the 1973 energy crises so that "fuel efficient" cars were just beginning to come off of the production lines. We must have driven back and forth across the country over a dozen times during our three years on the road. When we did settle down for a month or two at a time, Colorado and North Carolina seemed to be our favorite stomping grounds.

In fact, North Carolina was the location of another memorable event. Camille and I had been on the road for about two years and, as happens with most couples, the subject of marriage crept into our conversation every now and then. We did not specifically talk about Patti, but my ongoing legal relationship to her was an unspoken wall between us.

Simply stated, marriage to Camille was not possible as long as I was still married to Patti. Therefore, I filed for divorce in late 1979. The state of New Jersey (which was where Patti and I were married) allowed for an uncontested divorce decree when somebody had been physically separated from his or her spouse for eighteen months. The deserted spouse had no choice in the matter.

I did a great disservice to Patti by literally abandoning her, and I learned years later of Patti's heartfelt belief in my eventual return. Even after the divorce papers were finalized, she was faithful to wait another eight years with the hope of our marriage being reconciled.

My faithfulness, though, was soon to be pronounced to Camille. On April 26, 1980, I married this beautiful woman whom I had fallen in love with. In a small ceremony surrounded by family and friends, we walked down the aisle of the Pentecostal Holiness Church in Greensboro, North Carolina. My heart was "leapin" to the tune of "Here Comes The Bride … My bride, Camille."

As a lawful couple now, Camille and I spent our honeymoon at the Tropicana Hotel in Las Vegas, Nevada, where the 1980 World Classic 8-Ball Championship was being held. The first place prize was $25,000 and I had advanced into the final brackets with only eight players remaining in the tournament. If I won my next match against Jimmy Reid, I would face Mike Massey in the semifinals.

Mike and I had played together in many of the same tournaments since I had first seen him talking about Jesus at the Baton Rouge, Louisiana, tournament and I had come to consider Mike as my friend. Maybe it was his boldness in speaking about the God who I had rejected years before or possibly it was my admiration about this man's pool playing prowess, but I was feeling uncomfortable about beating Mike should I meet him in the semifinals.

My pool playing friends are probably rolling their eyes due to my confidently boasting about my ability to take Mike down in the semifinals should I have to play him. This is because they know billiard history. Mike would eventually be voted as one of the best, if not *the* best, artistic pool and trick shot artists of all time.

Mike was good and everybody liked Mike! In fact, they still like Mike.

When the question is asked, "Who is the most famous male American Pool Player?" the answer from many people would be *Michael "Mike" Massey*, alias "Tennessee Tarzan." He has won professional, national, and international tournaments in all of the billiard disciplines such as nine-ball, eight-ball, straight pool, one pocket, artistic pool and trick shots. Since the late 1970's, Mike has influenced the sport significantly as an accomplished player, instructor, consultant, and fund raiser. In 2005, Mike Massey was inducted into the Billiard Congress of America Hall of Fame and his accomplishments read like a novel including his winning multiple ESPN TV World Trick Shot titles as well as being a four time World Artistic Pool Champion.

In addition to Mike's many tournament titles, he has some of the following fun achievements on his resume:

* High run of 224 balls in straight pool.
* 11,230 balls pocketed in marathon shooting (24 hours)

* 8,090 balls pocketed in marathon shooting with one arm.
* World record for most racks of nine-ball run in a 24-hour period: 330 racks on live television in Austria.[11]

Mike is one of the few billiard professionals to also moonlight as an actor. He has appeared in movies such as "Pool Hall Junkies" with Chazz Palminteri, Ricky Schroder, and Christopher Walken, as well as "The Night The Lights Went Out In Georgia" with Kristy McNichol and Dennis Quaid. Mike has even played or taught pool with many celebrities such as Sugar Ray Leonard, Johnny Cash, Billy Bob Thornton, Scott Baio, Paul Sorvino, Jennifer Tilly, David Arquette, and others.[12]

In 1980, though, when Mike and I were competing for the world title and $25,000 prize, Mike was still just at the beginning of his prominent career. Most of his credentials were yet to be written so that, yes, I had the confidence to beat him. However, my perception of Mike went beyond his ability to offer me a competitive challenge. I looked to Mike as my spiritual leader of sorts and I expected him to mirror the integrity of the God who he publically proclaimed. I respected Mike and I was strangely drawn to the spiritual message he stood for. Within my own life, I found myself watching more Sunday morning televangelists, reading the Gideon Bibles found in the hotel nightstand drawers, and even talking to this Deity who must be out there somewhere if I was to believe what the televangelists and the Bible proclaimed.

Returning to my story, the night before my match with Jimmy Reid, I was unable to sleep. The clock had ticked its way to about four in the morning while I exasperatedly tossed and turned in our Tropicana king size bed. Camille was asleep beside me completely oblivious to my insomnia and as much as I wanted to wake her up to share my alertness, I resisted. Instead, I chose to dialogue with God.

"Well God," I began my oration, "I remember the light on the ceiling in 1976 and I still don't know what to make of it. Next, I joined the Navy where I really messed up. Then I met Camille and we threw our drugs away and straightened out our lives. We've been really seeking you, but to be honest, God, I'm confused. Who are you and what do you want me to do? I'm following you, Lord. I'm trying to follow you."

The thought never occurred to me that the God who I was attempting to follow might be the same God who I had known in my youth. Remember, I was raised in a fundamentalist evangelical church where the basic theological premise was, "Jesus loves me this I know for the Bible tells me so." However, I had rejected the religion of my mother and father because I figured belief in God had to be more sophisticated. Like most, I had to find God for myself. Little did I realize the simplicity of God's message. Jesus did love me and the Bible did tell me so.

Even though my prayer hinted at my desire to follow God, I was on my own journey. I was 30 years old. I was at the Tropicana Hotel, I was in the final eight of the world championship and I was going to possibly play Mike Massey. With my thoughts now steering toward this current matter, I continued my conversation.

"God, I don't know if I will have the heart to beat Mike if we draw each other in the semi-final match because he is playing pool for you now. I'm trying to follow you, God, like Mike Massey is following you..."

Upon uttering those words, a beam of light came through the window shade, made a left hand turn, pierced straight through my body and exited through the door. From the top of my head to the bottom of my feet, a warm energy overwhelmed me just like in 1976 when that other light entered my body. Once again I simply avowed, "There is a God."

Now for those readers who are leery of these supernatural events happening in my life, this is the last one which you will have to skeptically ponder. Technically, however, Camille can attest to the legitimacy of my claim because, just as this light beam was exiting through the door, she jumped up out of her sound sleep and exclaimed, "What was that? What was that in the room?"

With a curious calmness, I replied, "Don't worry hon. That was God."

As if it was nothing out of the ordinary for God to go passing through our room at four o'clock in the morning, Camille said, "Ohhhhh," and fell right back to sleep.

70

I was still wide awake, however. Whatever these encounters were in my life, this last one was a re-enactment of the light on the ceiling in 1976 because I experienced the same feeling, the same visual, and I responded with the same question.

"Okay God! What do you want me to do! Here I am. You did it again. What do you want me to do?"

Upon repeating the question, my mind immediately recalled what I had said just before the light beam entered and exited the room. "I'm trying to follow you, God, like Mike Massey is following you."

There it was. My clue!

Immediately before the light went through me, I had spoken of Mike Massey. "Of course! This has something to do with Mike. I have to call Mike Massey!"

With a complete disregard for the fact that it was four o'clock in the morning and everyone was sleeping, even the sun, I picked up the phone. Calling the Tropicana front desk, I asked to be connected to Mike Massey's room. He answered the phone.

"Mike, I'm sorry for calling you so early."

"Oh, it's alright Steve, I'm awake. What is it? What's up?"

"Mike, I've gotta talk to you. Please, can I talk to you?"

"Sure. I'll meet you down in the hotel lobby in five minutes."

Even as I hung up the phone, my mind was still trying to figure out what was going on. I must be on the right track because Mike was already up at four in the morning. God must be planning to speak to me through Mike! Mike must be the messenger from God who will explain what this whole light thing is about.

Now I was excited. Circumstances were beginning to mysteriously make sense and the pieces of the jigsaw puzzle were seemingly starting to fit together. At least my mind could see a possible interpretation of the transpired events. With soul stirring excitement, I hurried downstairs to meet Mike in the lobby. A few minutes after my arrival, Mike emerged from the elevator and saw me hovering nearby waiting for him. As we found a place to sit down, Mike began the conversation.

"So what's going on, Steve? What's up?"

Mike and I were friends. In fact, Mike had recently offered me a job working at his pool room in Chattanooga, but I had declined.

Our conversations had never taken a deeply personal turn even though we had enjoyed some good talks about both the Bible and billiards. Mike knew nothing of my past and certainly nothing about my unexplainable encounters. I had not shared my experiences with anyone for fear of skeptical reactions. Now was my opportunity to find out what these strange "light" phenomena meant because the light in my room had led me to Mike, who, because he was a man of God, must be a spokesman for God too. Thus began my babbling.

"Mike, you're not going to believe this. I had a light go through my body back in 1976 after I heard you talk about Jesus in Baton Rouge, Louisiana. I joined the Navy and then I met you again in North Carolina and told you about how I had straightened up my life. I married Camille last month and then, less than ten minutes ago, I'm up in my room wide awake talking my life through with God and as soon as I say, 'I'm trying to follow you, God, like Mike Massey is following you,' a light goes through my body again. What's going on, Mike? Tell me, what's going on?"

Mike began to cry! He looked at me sorrowfully with tears rolling down his cheeks and said, "I know what it is."

"Well, tell me! What's going on!"

"Steve, I've got to tell you the truth."

"The truth? What's the truth?"

"Steve, you know everything I have been telling you about Jesus? I haven't been living it. I'm a hypocrite."

"What are you talking about Mike?"

"Oh, I started out right. When you heard me speak in 1976, I was sincere and I was living for Jesus, but then I began to backslide as I became a celebrity. I've been living a secret life of sin. I have not been faithful to Jesus. I'm ashamed of who I have become."

I looked at him. Bewilderment was casting a long shadow over my expectation of Mike delivering God's message because here sat the supposed messenger confessing his failure to be the loyal ambassador for the God he claimed to serve. A righteous indignation brewed within me. The pedestal on which I had placed this man began to crumble. My limited Bible knowledge swelled

72

into a wave of confutation and I found myself in the reverse role of playing the messenger.

"Wait a minute, Mike. Wait a minute. This Jesus. I know this Jesus, too. I was taught about Him when I was little. I know Jesus saves and I know Jesus forgives. I remember memorizing a verse when I was a child. It said something like, 'If we confess our sins, He is faithful and just to forgive us our sins and to cleanse us from all unrighteousness.' I know this verse and others like it because I had to memorize probably a hundred verses for Sunday school by the time I was twelve years old. Mike, you can talk to Jesus and ask Him to forgive you and He will make you clean. You can go on from here and be the witness who you claim to be!"

Mike looked at me with sadness and said, "I can't. My faith is too weak."

Annoyed even further by his lame admission, I decreed, "Then you *are* a hypocrite and you will suffer the consequences."

Silence settled between us until Mike spoke again in an attempt to salvage our friendship. "I'm sorry, Steve. I know I've let you down. I wish I knew the answer you were looking for, but I'm at a loss, too. I don't know how to help other than to be your friend. I still would enjoy working with you, though, so that if you and Camille decide to settle down soon, I hope you'll consider taking the job in Chattanooga."

That was it? That was my supposed message from God? An offer to go to Chattanooga, Tennessee, and work for a man who did not even practice what he preached? Forget it. With the memory of my recent light experience now clouded over with my overall disappointment with Mike, I emotionally detached myself from this man who I had once admired.

Condemningly, I answered, "Thanks, but no thanks. Knowing what I know now, I couldn't work with you. In fact, I hope we win our next matches because if we play each other in the next bracket, I am going to destroy you on the pool table."

That was it. That was how it ended between Mike and me because we did not have to see or play each other in the semi-finals. Mike lost his next match and I was actually on the way to winning my next match until Jimmy Reid got out on an incredible shot. He was faced with a three rail kick shot in order to pocket the eight ball (which statistically is like a 1 in 50 shot) and he made it.

Appropriately, Jimmy not only beat me, but went on to win the 1980 World Classic 8-Ball title and the $25,000. I use the word "appropriately" because Jimmy is truly a money player. Throughout his career, he holds more than 40 billiard titles, but he is also recognized with a unique distinction by his peers. Listen to what Jimmy shares on his website:

> In 1994, at the men's pro billiards tour competing for the 'Lexington All Star 9-Ball Championship,' the audience, unbeknownst to me, had urged a group of my peers to vote on who they thought was the best money player.
>
> Almost all of the top ranked pool players over the previous 5 to 25 years were there, Johnny Archer, Francisco Bustamante, Wade Crane, Kim Davenport, Roger Griffis, Buddy Hall, Allen Hopkins, Bob Ogburn, Efren Reyes, Mike Sigel, Earl Strickland, Nick Varner, and C.J. Wiley, just to name a few.
>
> At the time, they were, without a doubt, a group of the best and most respected pocket billiard players in the world. And these great players voted yours truly, Jimmy Reid, as: *'The Best Money Player In The World For The Previous 25 Years, From 1969 through 1994.'* The next day Buddy Hall said to me, 'That's over a quarter of a century man."
>
> Of All Things, This I Am Most Proud.[13]

Jimmy Reid did have the tenacious ability to step up to the pool table and win the match when there was good money at stake. I am glad my loss helped Jimmy to earn this distinctive honor. However, I was now out of the tournament and I was angry. This whole Mike Massey incident had really set me off. My only satisfaction in the situation was seeing Mike lose too. Misery loves company and vengeance is sweet.

CHAPTER 10

"You can make many plans,
but the Lord's purpose will prevail."
(Proverbs 19:21)

Camille and I left Las Vegas (ironically nicknamed "The City of Lights"). As if I did not already have enough emotional scars, now I felt like my spiritual backbone had been dislocated. I wanted to know God, but I did not want to be deceived. Mike Massey had disappointed me and yet, unlike many people who reject God because they have been disillusioned by hypocrites, I found my soul still sincerely searching for the truth. I wanted to know about the lights. I wanted to know about God. I wanted to know what He wanted from me.

Obviously, I wanted a lot, but I was getting nothing, so I just kept doing what I had been doing. I continued to play pool. After a pilgrimage through California, Arizona, Colorado, Montana, and many other states offering players a place to potentially profit from their pool performance, Camille and I found ourselves back in Greensboro, North Carolina, competing in a tournament.

My performance had not been at its best since leaving Las Vegas, thereby causing a dwindling effect on our savings. I really needed a victory in order to fill up the coffer again.

The day was Saturday. If I could just win one more match, then I could come in on the next day, Sunday, and play in the money rounds. However, I lost. Inexplicably, my arm locked up again like it did back at the U.S. Open 9-Ball tournament in Norfolk just before Camille arrived and we began our three year odyssey of traveling around the country.

With nothing to do now on Sunday because I was out of the tournament, Camille and I decided to attend the church where we had been married many months before. When we arrived, the service was already in progress.

I had only conversed with the minister briefly on our wedding day. He knew of my pool playing profession, but he did not know anything about my life or what I had been doing.

Camille and I had just taken our seats when the pastor stopped his sermon and pronounced, "I have just received a word from the Lord for somebody out there in the congregation." Not being too familiar with the charismatic church, I chuckled at such a creative way to grab everyone's attention. The pastor reiterated his point to nobody in particular, but with the conviction as if it was to somebody in particular.

"I have just received a word from the Lord for someone in the congregation. The Lord is telling me that there is a person here who has been called to go to a certain city in this country. But he is not going. Instead, he is rejecting it. He is fighting the call and yet he needs to go. This person needs to come up to the altar and get on his knees and say 'Yes, I'll go.'"

My thoughts were spinning. We had just walked in and sat down. This man knew very little about me and yet, within minutes of our arrival, he had stopped his sermon to declare a supposed "word from the Lord" which fit my life and addressed what had been bothering me since my confrontation with Mike Massey.

As much as I disliked what Mike was doing, I could not get his Chattanooga, Tennessee, job offer out of my mind. After my string of losses, a job was looking pretty good, even if the job was working for a hypocrite. In fact, if my arm had not locked up during yesterday's tournament, then I would not even be sitting here in church.

This thought shook me up just as much as the preacher's declaration. My arm locking up the first time had led me to a three year venture with Camille. Did God allow my arm to lock up the second time in order to get me here in church? Did God have that light come through my Las Vegas hotel room so that I would call Mike? And did Mike offer me the job in Chattanooga again because God knew that I would be out of money soon? Was God breaking through my stubbornness to accept a job through this utterance, *"The Lord has something to say to someone in the*

77

congregation," and that someone was me? The emissary of God continued to reiterate his message.

"The Lord is telling me that there is somebody in this congregation who is to go a certain city, but he is refusing to go. God is telling this man to put away his unyielding spirit and to listen to what God is telling him to do. This person needs to be obedient to the Lord and come up to the altar and humbly say 'Yes, I'll go."

My heart was pounding and my head was pulsating with thoughts of Mike Massey and Chattanooga, Tennessee. Mike Massey had invited me to work with him in Chattanooga and I had stubbornly refused to go. Instead I told him, "Knowing what I know now, I couldn't work with you." Mike's invitation would not quit repeating itself in my mind and now here was this preacher up there pronouncing that *"Somebody needs to come forward and tell the Lord that he is going to go."*

I went. I stood up from my seat and I walked up to the front. Camille followed. I knelt down and, as Camille got on her knees alongside of me, she whispered, "Steve, what's going on?"

"Weren't you listening to what the preacher just said?"

"Well, yeah, but what has that got to do with us?"

"Camille. He was talking to us. That's us! We need to go to Chattanooga and take Mike up on his job offer despite what happened. God is calling us to go to Chattanooga."

"Okay. If it's God, I guess we should go. I mean, where else are we going to go? We're just traveling around anyway."

After the church service, we did go. We packed up the car, left Greensboro, North Carolina, and drove straight to Chattanooga where we rented a hotel room for one week.

Supposedly knowing God's will, I confidently set off to Mike's pool room appropriately called "Mike Massey's Billiards," and announced my purpose in coming.

"Hi, Mike. I've considered what you said, and I am here to accept your job offer."

"Steve. That was months ago. I'm sorry, but we hired someone else for the position."

"Don't you have anything for me?"

"It's not only my decision. I have two other partners who have a say in the matter."

What was I going to do now? From the looks of it, Mike really did have a thriving business. I briefly considered pleading my case to his two partners, Phil Windham and Dewey Boyd, but instead I chose to take what I felt was a more influential approach.

"Mike. You have to have something for me because God is the one who told me to come here."

"Really?"

"Yeah! I was in a church in Greensboro and the preacher was saying that God wanted someone in the congregation to go to a certain city. After our last talk, I kept thinking about your invitation for me to come here to Chattanooga and I immediately knew God was calling me here. How could there not be a job?"

"I'm sorry, Steve, but there's not."

Bewilderment mixed with a pinch of embarrassment summed up the recipe of my emotions right about then. Less than an hour before, I had been confidently following God's path, but now the trail before me was leading into a black forest. I was lost. If God did not want me here in Chattanooga, then where did He want me?

For the next week at least, I was to remain in Chattanooga. We had paid for a one week hotel rental and we could not afford to frivolously walk away. In fact, I could not even attempt to bring in some income by playing pool because my arm was still locked up. These circumstances allowed Camille and me plenty of time to discuss what we were going to do next. We chose to head back to Colorado because we had friends there who frequently sponsored us.

When our last day at the hotel arrived, Camille had our car packed and she had already crawled into her little perch in the back seat. The car engine was running and, in typical human nature fashion, I went back to the room "one last time" to make sure we had not forgotten anything.

As soon as I walked into the room, the phone rang. I remember thinking, "Boy. Whoever is calling just caught me in the nick of time." This was back in the days before cell phones. Once I was back on the road again, reaching me by phone or any other method was very difficult. However, because no one usually knew where we were, I figured the front desk clerk was calling to confirm our check out.

"Hello?"

"Steve, I'm glad you haven't left yet." Obviously it was not the hotel clerk.

"Hi, Mike. We are just about ready to leave. The car is packed and the engine is running. We're heading to Colorado."

"Don't go yet. I think I have something for you and my partners agree. Can you come down and talk with us right away?"

"Sure. We'll be right down."

Without even having to lose a moment to turn the key in the ignition, I jumped in the car and told Camille on the way about the "almost missed" phone call.

We arrived at Mike Massey's Billiards in record time. Just one week ago I had proudly walked into this pool room knowing that there was a job waiting for me. Today, I found myself humbly walking into this pool room knowing that there was a job waiting for me. I saw Mike and his two partners seated over at a corner table.

"Hi, Steve. I'm glad we caught you before you left."

"Yeah, me too. What's up? What do you have for me?"

One of Mike's partners began to speak. "Well, here is our thought. We want to promote professional pool tournaments right here in downtown Chattanooga at the Sheraton Hotel. We want to have all of the best players in the world come here. We want Mike to be the promoter and we want you to be the director. In addition, we want you to run some pool leagues and teach lessons in between events. What do you think, Steve?"

"That sounds great. Count me in."

For the first time in years, I had a job. Camille and I felt like we had a home. God had led us to Chattanooga.

Mike Massey and I became a team. Our first premier tournament held at the Sheraton Hotel was a landmark success capturing national attention. We filled the field with sixty four of the top players in the country. Up until then, an event of this magnitude had never been held in that part of the country. Yes, there had been the Las Vegas tournaments, Chicago tournaments,

80

New York tournaments, and the old Johnston City tournaments, but organized pool had now arrived in Tennessee.

True to the business plan, other pro tours spun off after this first big tournament. Additional promoters and sponsors offered to become involved, and Mike and I became road partners. Mike was the front man, or promoter, and I was in the background organizing, running pool leagues, directing, teaching, and doing the administrative duties. We traveled the country together competing in pool tournaments and winning our fair share of prize money. Mike would sing his country songs while driving down the highways (yes, Mike likes to sing!) and we both basically had a great time meeting a lot of different people and reminiscing.

Mike and I became good friends, but Mike was still living a dual lifestyle. Remember, I had grown up living my own dual lifestyle from high school through my Navy days. I understood the futility of this existence which might explain my vehement reaction when Mike had confessed his faults to me in Las Vegas. I was looking for my own anchor in life and seeing Mike's hypocritical choices caused me to look for a buoy elsewhere.

I believe God honored my searching heart because He soon crossed my path with a man who helped me to put my supernatural encounters into perspective. Whenever Mike and I were not on the road, my duties included giving pool lessons. One of my students was Buddy Scallia, a little Italian shoemaker who really loved the Lord. His outspoken relationship with God appealed to me, and we became pool room friends.

One night after we were done with our lesson, I shared my stories with him about the lights entering my body. I was not in the habit of telling people these stories. I had told Mike and the outcome of that scenario had gone south (literally!). However, I felt safe in confiding my intimate life to this man who seemed to be sincere in his faith. I really wanted to know who God was and what He wanted me to do.

After hearing my experiences, Buddy shared a passage of scripture which sparked a turning point in my spiritual journey. He took a Bible out of his pocket and said, "Steve, listen to this verse from Ephesians 6:12. 'For we wrestle not against flesh and blood, but against powers and principalities, against spiritual wickedness in high places, against rulers of the unseen dark domain.'"

My ears were tuned in at this point. During each of my encounters I had sensed a spiritual power beyond my earthly understanding. Apparently, the Bible had something to say about the supernatural.

Buddy continued, "Steve, right now we are surrounded with another dimension called eternity. Demons and angels exist within this other dimension and they are vying for your attention. The demons are trying to get you to follow Satan and the angels are trying to lead you to Jesus Christ. However, Steve, you must understand this important fact: *God allows you to have the choice of who you are going to follow.* You can choose if you are going to follow God or Satan. And this Book" (he picked up the Bible and held it within my view) "will lead you to Jesus Christ. You will get all of the answers to all of your questions if you will put your faith in what this Book says. It's in this Book, Steve. All of your answers are in this Book. Jesus Christ is the Lord of the universe and He has allowed these events in your life so that you will choose to place your faith in Him."

Here I had been searching for God since the light in the room in 1976, and yet I had not really been reading the Bible. When Buddy Scallia said, "It's in this Book, Steve. All of your answers are in this Book," I had a glimpse of understanding. The proverbial light bulb went on inside of me and I thought, "He's right!"

The Bible had always been the basis for believing when I was introduced to God as a child years ago in Sunday school. The God of the Bible had been my parents' God, Bobby Richardson's God, and Billy Graham's God. Maybe I could find this powerful and personal God in the Bible too?

As I started to read the Bible, I began to find answers to the questions which had been accumulating within me for years. God was beginning to teach me about Himself through His Word.

Reading and devouring the Bible became my hobby. Whenever Mike and I were on the road, I spent two or three hours a day reading. Many times Mike asked about what I was reading and we would actually talk together about spiritual things. We both knew better than to bring up the topic of hypocrisy, and yet the combination of Mike's repressed desire to once again serve God and my desire to openly begin serving God allowed us both to be confronted with what God had to say.

My desire to walk more closely with God made it increasingly more obvious that Mike was continuing to stray further away from God. During the course of our two years together, I observed Mike's life gradually sliding downhill. Having laid aside my anger at Mike for disappointing me in Las Vegas, my heart now went out to him because he had become my friend. I shared his pain as he struggled with both a deteriorating marriage and a deteriorating business. As a bystander, I saw the root of Mike's troubles really did go back to what he had said to me. Because Mike would not give up his secret lifestyle, he was at war within himself and those internal battles were taking a toll on him. Mike's world was starting to crumble and these falling crumbs were little by little eroding our relationship.

In hindsight, the local press instigated the upcoming rivalry which would eventually lead Mike and me down separate paths. Due to our many tournament titles, the two big newspapers in Chattanooga began to editorialize on who was the better player, Mike Massey or Steve Lillis?

Of course, Mike was the favored "home boy" in these articles (after all, he was "Tennessee Tarzan") and I was portrayed as the enemy from the north "leapin" down to prove himself in the south. The two publications were pitting us against each other. One paper declared Mike was the better player and the other tabloid countered with questions of whether Steve was really the better player. The hype warranted a response and since I was painted as the intruding underdog, I found myself in the position of publicly challenging Mike to a duel, a pool duel.

Ironically, the event impairing our partnership was held in the same Sheraton Hotel where two years earlier we had successfully launched our first landmark tournament. The advertised affair was a $5000 "winner take all" challenge match between Mike and me. Publicly, this rivalry appeared to be just another staged publicity stunt. Privately, this match represented more. As competitors, Mike and I had always bantered back and forth about who was the better player and we had a healthy respect for each other's game. But our game was not the issue. Our lifestyle differences were at odds, and this dissension fueled our determination to triumph.

The match was a race to 40 games of 9-Ball. The crowd had paid $5.00 a person to attend and we definitely gave them their money's worth. Although some may have thought we fixed the match in order to feed the reporters more fodder, trust me, we did not. Mike and I were playing for a very high stake: our integrity. We proved our point to each other because we played the match all the way to hill hill. (The double printing of the word *hill* is not a typographical error, but rather billiard cue sport terminology referring to a match up situation where both players are "on the hill" and the outcome of the next game will determine who will get kicked off of the hill and who will remain victoriously on the hill). In layman's terms, our score was tied at 39-39 and the race was to 40. Only one game stood between victory or defeat.

The crowd was on the edge of their seats when I walked up to break the rack for our last decisive game. The cue ball forcefully slammed into the clustered balls scattering them every which way and not one of them found its pathway to a pocket. I paused and analyzed the position of each ball on the table, searching to see if Mike would be able to run the table. Before I even sat down, I knew that he could. He did and I lost.

Mike might have won the match, but he was soon to lose his stability in life. Within a couple of years, Mike's life would go into a tail spin of depression as his once successful business ventures folded and his marriage failed.

As for me? I might have also spiraled into the depths of despair, as I usually did after a major loss, except I was offered another job within just a few short weeks after the headlines probably read,

"Mike Massey Shoots Down Steve Lillis."

It was a good time for me to "Get Out Of Dodge."

CHAPTER 11

"With narrowed eyes, they plot evil;
without a word, they plan their mischief."
(Proverbs 16:30)

Interestingly, a press release written on September 3, 2009 relates back to a job opportunity offered to me shortly after my loss to Mike. The American Business Defense and Advisory Council, at an event held in Washington D.C., announced the following:

> Entrepreneur, business owner, and land developer George Frank has been named 2009 Entrepreneur of the Year representing Montana.
>
> From humble beginnings during childhood that included being a newspaper carrier, Frank began his successful business career as a billiard lounge operator and professional pool player. Over the course of 50 years, Frank has created numerous businesses across the United States and has created jobs for several thousand people.
>
> In the late 1960's, he created and opened the first Corner Pocket billiard lounge in Billings that spawned Corner Pockets of America, Inc., a national billiard franchise company...
>
> 'My entire business career is marked by taking risks.' George Frank states. 'Because of that, I've made some business mistakes. But when I see opportunities, I enjoy working hard and hiring good people to turn ideas into successful business realities.'[14]

You might be wondering how this news account relates to my story. I was one of the people hired by George Frank. In fact, I like the accuracy of his statement above because, after you read my side of the story, you will discover that, with respect to one of his ventures, I was the one *taking the risks.* I was the one saving his franchise from becoming a *business mistake.* I was the one *working hard.* I was the one firing the bad people and hiring the *good people* in order to turn one of his franchise locations into a *successful business reality.*

Given what George and I both know now about the job offered to me, we would probably rewrite his opening script to recite the popular line:

"Your mission, Steve, should you decide to accept it, is..."

After accepting his job offer, Camille's and my life did almost self destruct in feelings of frustration and helplessness. The truthfulness of Buddy Scallia's scripture verse about "spiritual wickedness in high places" applied itself directly to our circumstances.

However, the saga about to unfold was not George's fault. God prompted him to call the right man for the right job and we remain good friends today because of this realization.

Camille and I had met George Frank, the Corner Pockets proprietor, and his wife Judy a few years earlier during the summer of 1979 when we had chosen to stay in Billings, Montana, for a couple of months in order to cool down and escape the sweltering heat scorching the surrounding states. After we left, we had continued to stay in touch so that George was up to date with my job responsibilities and my recent enjoyment of lengthy Bible discussions. In other words, when George called me a few weeks after my hill hill match against Mike, I was not really surprised. However, the content of our conversation created some curiosity.

"Hi, Steve. This is George."

"Hey George. How are you doing?"

"Well. I'm doing great spiritually! I recently became a Christian and got saved."

"Praise the Lord! It sounds like some of our conversations about God got you to thinking."

"They actually did. And they also got me thinking about who would be the best person to help with some management difficulties I'm having at my Las Vegas Corner Pocket's franchise. You keep coming to mind."

"Me? Why?"

"Because I need someone I can trust to go in and straighten things out. This is my showpiece location where I walk through potential buyers and yet business losses have continued to increase in either merchandise or damages to the property."

"Ouch! That's not good. What's going on?"

"I don't know, Steve. That's why I want you to go to Las Vegas and look it over and consider becoming my General Manager. If you have an interest, then afterwards I will fly you back here to Billings so that we can talk through the particulars."

"Okay, George. I'll go take a look."

Within a couple of weeks, Camille and I arrived in Nevada. I still remember walking into the Las Vegas Corner Pockets like it was yesterday. The franchise was beautiful! It had a fully equipped bar, fine dining, a good pro shop, and an array of slot machines. Catering to the elite was a private chamber called "The King's Billiard Room" which was graced with elegant pool tables, chandeliers, exquisite portraits, plush carpeting, and stately throne chairs. The main billiard room sported thirty pool tables which were maintained to an immaculate standard. Did I mention the beauty of this franchise? Of course I was interested in managing this jewel!

Upon communicating my willingness to accept the position, George flew me back to his home in Montana. Through our discussions, he not only offered me a salary greater than what I had ever earned in my life, but he also offered to hire Camille as my assistant manager.

Despite these financial bells and whistles, though, I felt a moral obligation. George had approached me in the name of the Lord. He was a brother reaching out to me in the billiard industry who wanted my help and I would put forward my best efforts. The value of lost merchandise and damages to the property was substantial. Employees with destructive motives would need to be confronted and I was determined to ferret out these criminals. I had been reading the Bible faithfully now for almost two years. I felt like I had reached a spiritual identity where I knew who I was in Christ. Little did I know about the violent storms ahead which would require my faith to serve as my anchor.

George and I prayed together and then I traveled back to Las Vegas. The night before I was to begin my first day of work, I walked out onto the desert stretching out behind our apartment. A cool breeze was blowing through the air. Camille and I had recently purchased a plaque which hung on our apartment wall and I remember meditating on its words quoting Psalm 27:1:

"The Lord is my light and my salvation,
whom shall I fear."

What an appropriate verse for me to ponder given my experiences. I knelt on the desert floor and committed the job to God. My fearful feelings fled as my faith found freedom to face whatever my Father was going to allow.

To fire or not to fire? That was my first question. Should I immediately fire every employee and start over or should I gradually find the problem people and let them go one by one? I chose the second option because it seemed easier and would minimize interruption to the regular flow of business. Time would tell if I made the wrong choice.

Thanks to the security cameras located throughout the building, I was able to watch and review what was going on from my downstairs office. Within the first six months, I discovered employees brazenly stealing from the company. Some were stealing from the slot machines by manipulating a wire into the mechanism thereby triggering the coin box to open up. Bar maids were giving away free drinks and waitresses were providing complimentary meals. Cue sticks and other billiard equipment were walking out of either the front door or the back door depending on whether the pro shop personnel felt like giving it away or stealing it. Even friends of our employees were getting in on the action!

One by one I began to terminate employees and I quickly learned the repercussions of my decisions. For each person I let go, one act of retaliation would follow. These were not just minor tit for tats. These were vindictive acts. For example, after I fired the first employee, the water main outside of the building was deliberately broken. I quickly began to understand George's statement of "We have experienced significant losses in either merchandise *or damages* to the property." Plumbers were just as expensive back then as they are now!

Electricians were pricey too. The electrical lines running into the building were severed shortly thereafter when I removed another corrupt employee. Each time I discovered a dishonest staff member, I fired him or her and then inevitably another act of vandalism would present itself.

Even new employees were crooked. I would get rid of one bad apple and another one wormed in to take his or her place. The old saying, "Two steps forward, three steps back," was an accurate description of my career path as I attempted to drain away the dirty pool of workers.

Plumbers. Electricians. Locksmiths. Cabinetmakers. Contractors. You name the profession and I probably spent money within their trade. The cash disbursements journal was filled with payments for "Repairs and Maintenance." Each check I wrote seemed to gaze up at me and sneer, "Are you ready to saddle up yet and get out of Dodge?" Of course, I had already left Dodge, remember? However, that was just a literary analogy. Here in Las Vegas, I really felt like I was a cowboy living in the wild west. My independent frontiersman nature therefore reared up and snorted back at the sneering check, "No. I'm going to ride this bucking business bronco out." Then, I would willfully rip the check out of its binding and send it off as if I had just roped a bull and put him in the cattle car heading out.

Basically, the price of releasing employees from their jobs was going to be repairing whatever damages ensued. After about ten months of my involvement with this cat and mouse game, I was still playing. In other words, I had not quit. I still held the position of General Manager which apparently was aggravating my subordinates. They wanted me gone and they soon let me know it.

The note read, "You keep this up and we will kill you." I found it stuck under the windshield wipers on my car which was now being supported by four viciously slashed tires. I had just relieved another person of his job, and this time my opponents upped the ante from mere property damage to threatening my life.

Admittedly, a tremble of fear went through me, but then I remembered the verse written on the plaque hanging on our apartment wall. Challenging myself with the same question as the psalmist, I asked, "The Lord is my light and salvation. Whom shall I fear?" As I pondered the verse, a thought struck me. I did not remember the plaque showing a question mark at the end of the sentence. The words were not written as a question, but rather as a statement of fact. "The Lord is my light and salvation. Whom shall I fear."

A righteous anger rose up within me as I carried out the obvious conclusion to the statement. With confidence and boldness I thought, "The Lord is my light and salvation. I will fear no man." If I had previously nurtured any inkling of giving up, this truth from God's Word motivated me to continue fighting the war. George had hired me to turn this Corner Pocket franchise back to a successful business entity and I was going to accomplish the task. No one was going to threaten me.

I was not prepared, though, for the assault to culminate in a threat to Camille's safety. She had caught a customer brazenly stealing a cue stick out of the display case and, like a mother bear protecting her cub, she tackled him right there at the store. I quickly called the police and, upon their arrival, we heatedly told the officers about what had happened. We knew this "customer" was most likely a friend and accomplice of one of our employees and, as managers, we demanded his arrest. However, one of the policemen dismissed our order with the response, "The jails are full and we only take people in for violent crimes." We stared back in disbelief. Another committed crime would go without consequence.

As if nothing even happened worth reporting in a man's life autobiography, the police sent the guilty customer on his way, and told us to go cool down. Sigh. I felt like I was alone in this fight. However, I was not alone as I would soon find out. God had been protecting the business as well as both of our lives. The police might not have wanted to get involved and write up a report, but the FBI was quite interested.

Unbeknownst to me, a satanic cult had infiltrated its members into many of the businesses along Boulder Highway on the west side of Las Vegas. As more information was released, I discovered the source of our problems. Our head bartender belonged to this cult and had been the ringleader behind all of the retaliatory acts occurring at our Corner Pockets. I had trusted this man and yet he had completely deceived me. Needless to say, I fired him. With this anti-leader now gone, my role as manager began to prevail as remaining workers either quit or submissively fell into line.

Profits immediately improved. When George sent some of his corporate men to Las Vegas after everything was running smoothly to give me my next mission, I willingly accepted. "Steve, profits are beginning to grow, business is starting to come around, you've done your job, and for your own health and safety, we need to get you out." Camille and I gratefully accepted a very generous severance pay and we wearily journeyed back to New Jersey where we spent some time licking our wounds at Camille's mother's home.

George called me up a few months later with an update. "The FBI busted up the cult. It had not only infiltrated our business, but a number of other businesses in the area. Thank you, Steve. God led me to the right man whom He knew would stand up against the spiritual wickedness attacking my business. I am grateful to both you and Camille for serving the Lord faithfully on my behalf. God bless you."

CHAPTER 12

"Zeal without knowledge is not good;
a person who moves too quickly may go the wrong way."
(Proverbs 19:2)

"If I knew then what I know now." How many of us look back at our lives and think the same thing? I wish I had understood the importance of a woman's need to feel safe and financially secure back when I was in my thirties. Especially when that woman was my wife and her need for adequate protection and provision became dependent on my ability to satisfy.

I had failed as a husband and I would continue to fail. Camille was very strained emotionally after our Las Vegas experience. Her need to feel safe had been violated by her defenseless, vulnerable exposure to the unpredictable vindictive acts against us and I had not been able to shield her. We had accumulated sufficient cash reserves, however, allowing me to offer her adequate provision. At least until I ended up taking that away from her also. I was ignorant. Very ignorant.

After a short stay in New Jersey, Camille and I returned to Chattanooga where we rented a cozy garden apartment, bought a new car, joined a health club, and settled into a seemingly normal life. At Camille's urging, we even added a new member to the family. A cute little dog named Punky.

I enrolled at the University of Tennessee for a semester and, of course, I continued to play professional pool in search of becoming a world champion. Returning to my old job with Mike was not an option. We traveled to some tournaments together, but he was spiraling downhill in depression. His business was deteriorating and a final divorce seemed imminent due to his wife leaving him and taking along their two children.

My heart broke with compassion and love for Mike as I watched him struggle over those next couple of years. He had been instrumental in helping me succeed as a professional pool player and yet the consequences of his unwise lifestyle were catching up to him. By early 1985, Mike ended up in a depression like the one I had struggled through back in 1976 and he did not want to leave the house. Lamenting life, he just sat in his porch rocking chair for hours staring into space. Remembering my own personal experience of what this loneliness was like, I went to his house and forced him to take walks in the park, gave him leg massages to help with the atrophy, and dragged him to church as many times as he would allow himself to be dragged.

I was now attending a local church and had built up a network of Christian friends. Studying the Bible and dialoguing about Scripture was still one of my favorite pastimes. I continued to provide pool lessons for many of my prior students and compete in pro tournaments via sponsorship money. With our bank account sufficiently stocked, earning a steady income was not necessary.

Camille felt a great sense of accomplishment in this because not too many pool players return from being road players with money in the bank. She had scrimped and budgeted every dollar which was now accumulated in our savings and she felt *secure*. There is that word again which held more value than I comprehended.

While Camille worked hard to protect our money, I became lazy because of our money. "Complacent" would have been a good word to describe my attitude. Over time, my commitment to practice diminished. My winning track record was gradually becoming tarnished by a losing streak and some of my backers were beginning to back off.

Becoming disgusted at my accumulated losses, I began searching for ways to motivate myself to win. My sponsors may have been losing faith in me, but I had not lost faith in myself. Searching for a solution, I contemplated becoming my own sponsor. I had been losing at pool because I had no pressure on me. With others footing the bill, I experienced no real consequence if I lost. Paying for my own expenses would impose pressure on me, thereby stimulating me to win.

After making the decision to sponsor myself, I next turned my thoughts toward where I would get the necessary money. Finding a job would have been a reasonable solution. The problem, however, was the likelihood of the work roster interfering with the out of town tournament schedule. No, working was not the answer.

An alternative strategy was to use our savings. The money was available and if I had earned it once, I could earn it again. The additional incentive to not lose our reserves would surely light a fire under me to start winning. Choosing to decline the sponsorships being offered to me, I began to break into our nest egg to pay my pool way.

Many of you, especially the women, can almost hear Camille's imploring cry, "Steve! No! Don't do it! We have worked so hard to get all of this money in the bank to have a good life. Don't do it Steve! Don't do it......"

But I did do it. I refused to listen because I had put my own goals and priorities ahead of my wife. The idolatry of pool had a grip on me and I did not recognize its power. I had covered my addiction with claims of rationalization. I was not living a double lifestyle like Mike and I was going to church. I was an honest decent pool player who was just trying to make a living at playing pool.

As you have probably already guessed, my self-motivating scheme fell short of reaching its goal of inducing me to win. I continued to play and I continued to lose. Now, though, every loss was eating away at our savings account which showed withdrawal after withdrawal in order to pay tournament fees, traveling expenses, hotel rates, and restaurant tabs. Camille's growing insecurity due to my irresponsibility prompted her to request us to move back to New Jersey near her family. However, housing was too expensive in New Jersey so that we compromised and moved near my parents in Pennsylvania. As a result, we had to give up Camille's beloved dog, Punky, because we could not find housing that would take pets. Needless to say, Camille was heartbroken which placed me directly in the doghouse.

We lived in Pennsylvania only a few months before we went completely broke. Sponsoring myself in pool proved to be as

94

stupid as representing myself in court. You know the old saying which actually has two versions, both of which are true:

"A man who represents himself has a fool for a client."
and
"A man who represents himself has a fool for an attorney."

Either way you look at it, I was a fool. Camille and I had been married legally for five years and we had been together for almost eight years. Earning that money had been a team effort and my seizing the autonomy to independently govern its expenditure was an act of larceny within our marriage. All of our savings, not to mention all of Camille's hard work of keeping our lifestyle on a sustainable budget, was gone. Our financial security had vanished. Foolishly, I had taken our life savings and dumped it back into playing pool. Was it any wonder that Camille felt like I had betrayed her?

In a feeble attempt to make it up, I went out and got a job working in a men's clothing store selling suits. I should have fitted myself for a straight jacket so that I could not inflict further harm on Camille. She was heartbroken and I did not understand to what extent until I came home from work one day and found a note on the kitchen table which read,

Steve, my sister came and I'm going back home to live with her and my mother. I took the car and I took my personal possessions. I left the furniture and the rest of the stuff is all yours. You can do with it what you want. Camille

I was devastated. My partner was gone. I knew Camille felt like I had deserted her by squandering our livelihood, but I had not anticipated her deserting me. She abandoned me just like I had abandoned Patti back in 1978. The truth of the old saying "Turnabout is fair play" stabbed me in the heart.

Painfully, I experienced the loss of the one who I had wanted to share my life with. I had become a one woman man and Camille was my woman. Yes, I had married Patti, my first wife, but I had not comprehended or cared about commitment then. Our marriage had been one of youthful indulgence and convenience due to both of us experiencing tremendous pressure from our parents to get married because we were already living together.

The difference between my marriage to Patti and my marriage to Camille was in my attitude. Being high on marijuana on our wedding day, I remember standing beside Patti at the altar and actually muttering under my breath, "I don't believe in this whole Catholic mass thing." My demeanor made a mockery of the whole marriage ceremony. In fact, my admission to Patti years later of my sanctimonious attitude provided partial grounds for approving her request for an annulment.

My union with Camille had been different. When I stood at the altar with Camille at my side, I believed in the sanctity of marriage. My vows before God were sincere and I meant every word. "For better or for worse, for richer or for poorer, in sickness and in health, till death do us part." I really loved Camille. When she walked out, her departure drove me to my knees. I knelt by my bed and prayed.

> *Lord, what do you want me to do? I have made a mess of my life. I have taken two women along with me on this journey and I have hurt both of them. I've only lived for myself. Because of my idolatry of pool and my wanting to be the greatest player in the world, I have not only lost all of our money, but I have lost Camille, my helpmate and my partner. I betrayed her, Lord. And since I don't know what else to do, I surrender right now to you. I surrender my heart. I surrender my life. I even surrender my cue stick.*

I reached for my treasured cue stick and I laid it on the bed as an offering.

> *Here God. Take my cue stick. I will not play this game ever again unless you tell me to. I'm done playing pool. It has ruined my life and only led me to make poor decisions. Here it is, Lord, take it.*

I got up off of my knees. No bells, no whistles, and no lights on the ceiling could be heard or seen. Instead, I felt a peace. A quiet assurance filled my heart. I felt as if I had, by an act of my will, crossed over into a place of complete obedience. With newfound confidence, I was willing to do whatever God wanted me to do from that day forward...no matter what.

CHAPTER 13

"My child, listen and be wise.
Keep your heart on the right course."
(Proverbs 23:19)

Statistically, many people move back home after a marriage breakup. According to the University of Michigan news service, spouses whose marriages ended during the 1980's had a 56 percent higher probability of returning home than those whose marriages ended before 1960.[15] The year was 1985 when Camille left me and we both proved the accuracy of the university's study. Camille went home to live with her mother and I found myself at my parents' doorstep.

According to this same report, education was also linked to the "return home" decision. Men or women with only a high school diploma and no college degree had the highest *risk* of returning home. Risk. An interesting choice of words. What would make home a "risky" place? My dad apparently knew the answer and responded accordingly.

Upon breaking the news of our separation to my parents, my mother compassionately responded, "Well Stephen, you can move back in with us. Your old bed is still in your room upstairs and you can stay as long as you need to."

My dad's counter proposal held the wisdom of a father. "Son, you are welcome to stay with us, but only for three weeks. After three weeks, you must leave. I will help you in whatever way I can, but you must go and find your own way and not stay here under our roof. Steve, your mother and I have given you everything. We have shown you the way to live. We have taught you God's principles and you have watched the pattern of our lives. With God's help, you can do this. You will make it, Son."

Some are applauding my father for his tenet of tough love while some are waiting to hear my mother's rebuttal since the female's maternal instincts would typically rebel against such a short time limit. Surprisingly, my mother yielded to my father's leadership in this matter and she remained silent. Although I wanted her to step forward and argue on my behalf, I knew my father's edict was right. I was thirty five years old and I had just spent most of the last eight years traveling like a gypsy. The road ahead was just going to be another life journey for me.

Securing transportation was going to be my first order of business. I had no car because Camille had taken our car. Of course, I would have had the old Pontiac Catalina if had I not sold it against Camille's wishes. Before we had moved up to Pennsylvania from Tennessee, I had the brilliant idea of selling the "extra" car in order to obtain tournament expense money. The Catalina was running phenomenally well even though it had over 150,000 miles on it. Camille pleaded with me, "Steve, don't sell the Catalina! We need two cars." Refusing to consider her input, I sold the car.

My parents helped me purchase an old inoperable car from my brother-in-law for two hundred dollars. Due to my being a pool player and not a mechanic, I could only stand by and watch my dear father's labor of love as he put in new brakes, new hoses, new belts, and whatever other new parts were required.

As the time drew nearer to my departure date, my parents both offered input as to what I should do. My mother's suggestion was to drive down to the PTL Club which was a ministry located in North Carolina. One of its outreaches was called "The Tent City." People who had nowhere to live, and yet felt called by the Lord to serve Him, had erected a tent city on the ministry's property where they could pray and seek God's guidance. My mother advised, "Stephen, go down to the PTL Club and live there and listen for what God wants you to do."

My father, on the other hand, said, "Son, do you have any other choices? Can you go get a job somewhere? Can you make a life for yourself?"

In response to his challenging tone, I put forward some alternative options. "Well, Dad, I've got my Navy veteran benefits and the GI Bill which will pay for me to go to school. I spent a semester at the University of Tennessee in Chattanooga and I could go back, earn my college degree, and probably find a job because I know a lot of people from when I lived there and worked for Mike Massey."

"Well, Son. That sounds like a good plan. Go back to school and get a job. But let me tell you, if you feel God's calling you to go to the Tent City, well, what am I going to say?"

Obviously my father was diplomatically allowing me to wisely consider my mother's opposing counsel. In his usual way, he was encouraging me to become my own judge and jury. I had heard the evidence and now it was my decision as to how I would proceed. In my typical fashion, I proceeded without a plan.

When my three weeks were up, I got in the car and started driving south on Route 81 directly toward a fork in the road which was just before the state of Tennessee. Choosing left at the interchange would take me to the PTL Club's Tent City in North Carolina and navigating right would lead me straight into Chattanooga, Tennessee, where I could go to school and get a job. My hands were tightly gripping the steering wheel and my thoughts were vacillating: "Do I go left which is my mother's suggestion or do I go right which is my father's advice? Left my mother. Right, my father. Left, my mother. Right, my father."

The fork in the road was quickly approaching and I honestly did not know which way to go. I could not choose between the voices of my mother and my father which were echoing within my heart. As I reached the last moment when a decision had to be made or I would crash into the divider, I inexplicably felt a tug to the right and my hands suddenly turned the wheel toward Chattanooga. A quick analysis of my emotions revealed my sense of peace. I must have made the right decision to go right.

Within two hundred miles, I arrived safely in Chattanooga. I drove straight to the University and walked directly to the Dean's Office. I did not have an appointment and I did not even know if I could enroll because the semester was starting in less than a week.

The dean agreed to see me. I walked into his office with complete ignorance about how I was going to educate this man on the benefits of accepting me as a student. I came straight to the point.

"Sir, can I come back to school?"

"How old are you, Son?" (I no longer carried my youthful luster).

"I'm 35 years old."

"You are 35 years old and you want to come back to school? Where are you going to live?"

"Sir, would you provide me a place in one of the dorms?"

"Let me understand this. You come in here right off of the street, want to get back into school at your age, live on campus because you have no place to stay, and you expect me to accommodate you?"

I looked at him, a fatherly figure with balding features, and confidently said, "Yes, sir. I will do anything. I'll work. I'll scrub floors. I'll wash windows. I'll take any kind of job on campus. I'll do whatever. I don't care where you put me. You can put me in any kind of dorm room. Anything you've got. Sir, I have nowhere to go, but I want to work and I want to finish my education. I know that I am 35 years old, but God has spoken to my heart and He wants me to make a new start in life."

The dean was contemplatively quiet. My school file had apparently been pulled prior to my entering his office because it was on his desk. He opened the jacket cover and began to look through pages which documented my prior school transcripts and personal history. With my life laid out in front of him like an open book, I sat quietly as I awaited my moment of truth.

"Steve, I'm going to give you a chance." The dean looked up and studied me further and, as if he was convincing himself of making a wise decision, he again said, "Steve, I'm going to give you a chance."

A silence cloaked the room as the dean pondered a plan. I knew better than to speak and I waited for him to outline his proposal.

"I'll tell you what. I can put you in the Freshman dorm, but you will be living among 18 and 19 year old kids. It's not the nicest dorm, but it's all I can do for you."

Before he could change his mind, I eagerly responded, "Yes, sir. I'll take anything. I don't care. Thank you, sir."

101

"You're welcome, Steve. My secretary will give you your enrollment forms and you can sign up for classes next week. As far as a job, check out the village mini market and put in an application. Your mature age and the fact you attended school here before might just land you a position. Good luck."

I left his office and went straight to the village mini market which was located on campus amidst the apartment style dorms. The dean's recommendation proved to be well-advised because I was offered a full time job as a cashier.

My life as a student began. During the day, I attended classes and did homework. At 4:00 in the afternoon I would go to the cafeteria and eat as much as would fit. Following my feeding frenzy, I would go to the village mini market and work from 5:00 until midnight where I would mingle with everyone who passed by my register.

Despite my self-centered nature, I really was a likeable guy. In fact, these kids broke through my protective barriers because, like them, I was a misfit trying to find where I might fit in life. Of course, I was the more obvious misfit which was a fact made evident to me through their light hearted bantering.

"Hey, old man! What are you doing here?"

Because I really had no clue what I was doing, I responded, "Jesus called me here. Praise the Lord and God bless you!" The kids did not know what to do with my response any more than I knew what to do with my response, but the slogans became a cashiering ritual.

"Hey, old man! What are you doing here?"

"Jesus called me here. Praise the Lord and God bless you!"

Even though my mind was being distracted by duties and my drive for a degree, the drama of my previous life did not easily detach itself from my feelings of dejection and despair over Camille's departure. In fact, my decision to put down my cue stick on the day I found her note was proving to be more difficult than I thought. From 1970 to 1985, I had spent over half of my waking moments playing pool. The game was ingrained in my mind. At night when I would lie in bed attempting to fall asleep, I could hear the click of the balls as they kissed against each other. The smell of the chalk dust infiltrated my temporal lobe and visions danced in my head of sparkling colored balls tempting me to send them to their pockets. Every fiber in me wanted to get up and go hit balls at a local pool room. I yearned to play pool, but the memory of how pool had ruined my marriage kindled my soul to cry out, "Oh God, please take away this addiction from me!"

My petition was answered by a full time job and full load of courses which kept my nose to the grindstone. Little by little, as the school year progressed, the lure to play pool subsided. What did not subside were my thoughts of Camille. I missed her more than I did pool. We had not kept in touch so that when I saw an envelope from her in the mail about midway through the semester, my heart leapt for joy with the hope of our reuniting. Without waiting to get back to my dorm, I sat down on a nearby bench and opened the letter immediately.

> *Dear Steve,*
> *I have met another man and we are planning to get married. I will be sending you the divorce papers soon. Please sign and return without putting up a fight. This is what I want. Camille*

I was stunned. Divorce was not what I wanted. Feelings of jealousy, anger, regret, sorrow, and loneliness surged through me. I sat in front of the university mailboxes for the longest time just staring at the letter in disbelief. My textbooks were sitting beside me and I noticed the Bible on top. I still read my Bible faithfully. Obviously reading and applying were two different things because I continued to hurt people and the person who I had hurt the most was Camille. I did not want to hurt her anymore and if not hurting her further meant releasing her from my life, then I would release her. I chose to sign the divorce papers without protest when they arrived.

The question of divorce nagged at me. As I read the Bible on the subject, questions began to arise. My relationship with Camille had begun in adultery. Were we living in an adulterous marriage? Was I married to Camille when I was not supposed to be? Was my marriage to my first wife, Patti, really my legitimate marriage and my second marriage not recognized by God? As I continued to read through the Scriptures, I began to question my marriage to Camille. For the first time in my life I thought, "Maybe what I did was sinful and I was wrong."

These thoughts prompted me to write Patti a letter asking for her forgiveness. Eight years had passed since I had abandoned her. I now understood the pain she must have endured when she opened the envelope containing our divorce papers.

Patti's quick response a few days later was unexpected and thought provoking. We had not communicated since before our divorce and yet Patti answered as if our marriage still had hope.

> *Dear Steve,*
>
> *Your letter was an answer to my prayers! Since you have been gone all of these years, I have become a Christian and I have been praying for God to reunite us. I never really accepted our divorce because I knew that your marriage to Camille was wrong. May we continue corresponding in search of what God's plan is through all of this?*
>
> *Still Yours, Patti*

My questions all seemed to find their answer within the context of this note. Learning about Patti's unspoken faithfulness to our marriage after years of separation softened my heart. I had not known she had been waiting. My emotions were jumbled. I had spent the last eight years on an adventure with Camille and Camille no longer wanted me. Maybe this was my opportunity to make my life right. Maybe I needed to undo what I did with Camille. I wrote back and shared my thoughts with Patti.

> *Dear Patti,*
>
> *I'm sorry I messed up our lives and I'm thinking you may be right. Maybe God does want me to come back to you and honor our marriage because that was my true marriage. Let's continue to pray and seek God's will.*
>
> *I will write again soon, Steve*

Thus began a series of letters between Patti and me. We shared, we grieved, and we hoped. With my Christmas school break approaching, we planned to rendezvous and discuss the possibility of getting remarried since Camille already had divorce proceedings under way. My life was once again beginning to make sense.

CHAPTER 14

"How can we understand the road we travel?
It is the Lord who directs our steps."
(Proverbs 20:24)

Upon taking my last final exam for the semester, I packed up the car and headed to my parents' home for Christmas. I was looking forward to sharing my news about Patti with them and I was also looking forward to seeing Patti. She must have been looking forward to seeing me too because when I arrived home my mother greeted me with a sly look on her face and said, "Guess who you got a phone call from?"

Of course, I knew who the phone call was from. With a cunning look of my own, I smugly answered, "Patti. I was expecting her call."

My mother had a strange look on her face. Apparently Patti had not told her why she had called so that I was still going to have the fun of announcing the news about our rekindled relationship. However, the look on my own face must have turned odd when I heard my mother say, "No, Stephen. It was Camille. Camille called. She wants to meet with you and her pastor at a church in New Jersey."

"Camille! She's supposed to be serving me divorce papers! Why is Camille calling me! She left me to go marry another man! And now she has a pastor? What's going on?" I was obviously hysterical.

Clueless about the underlying cause of my emotional outcry, my mother was tentative. "I don't know, Stephen, but she wants to meet with you right away. Here is the phone number where she can be reached."

I took the piece of paper and I walked to the phone in the kitchen where I could find some privacy. After two rings, I heard Camille's voice on the other end of the line.

"Hello?"

"Hi, Camille. It's me. My mother said you called?"

"Hi, Steve. Thanks for calling. I have some things to say and I want to say them to you with my pastor present. Can you meet me at my church here in Wyckoff?"

"What's this about, Camille? Why can't you just say what you want to say on the phone? What is it that you want?"

"Please Steve. It's not bad what I want to tell you. I just want my pastor with me when I do. Will you come? Please?"

I agreed to go and the next morning I drove the two hours to the Wyckoff Assembly of God Church in New Jersey. Camille was waiting for me in front and she looked uneasy. Questions swelled within me, but she was obviously too tense to communicate. The pastor invited us into his office and he was the first one to speak.

"Thanks for coming, Steve. Camille has asked me to speak to you on her behalf because she does not know how to say what she wants to say."

I turned my gaze from the pastor to Camille. I had no clue what she might have done or what she wanted to say, but she looked like a scared puppy huddled in the corner afraid of what might come next. Bewildered, I turned my attention back to the pastor who sensitively continued.

"I'll come straight to the point. Camille has repented from walking out on you. She has rededicated her life to Christ and she would like for you to forgive her. Camille is asking to be reconciled to you as your wife."

The pastor's words were cut short by Camille's interruption. Apparently, she wanted to confirm the truth of what he said before I got up and walked out. However, I could not have gotten up and walked out even if I had wanted to. I felt like a truck had run me over.

"The pastor is telling you the truth, Steve. I made a big mistake and I want to tell you what happened. Two weeks ago I was driving home after being out drinking and all of a sudden I felt like God was in the car. It was so real that I pulled over and stopped. I

107

heard Him in my heart saying, 'You've got to go back to your husband. You can't divorce him. You can't marry this other man. You've got to go back with Steve and live a Christian life. Don't throw this marriage away.'"

Camille paused to take a breath before continuing to plead. "That's what happened, Steve! I'm telling you the truth! Please let me come back and be your wife."

In disbelief, I looked back and forth between the two of them. I was already in the process of making plans to reunite my marriage with Patti and now Camille wanted me to reunite my marriage with her? Needless to say, I was perplexed. Having no clue how to respond, I asked for time.

"I don't know, Camille. I don't know, Pastor. I need to think this through. I'm confused."

"Of course," the pastor replied because Camille was once again too distraught to speak. "We understand and we will be praying for God to guide your decision."

Awkwardly, I left the meeting and drove back to Pennsylvania entreating God with one simple question. "What do you want me to do, Lord?"

Not knowing what to say, but knowing something had to be said, I called Patti. She immediately sensed there was something wrong by the tone in my voice.

"Steve, what's wrong?"

"I don't know, Patti. I'm confused. I arrived here at my parents' house and Camille had called with a message that she wanted to meet with me and her pastor. She wants us to get back together. I don't understand what's going on. What should I do?"

Patti's voice was tender. I heard both vulnerability and confident strength within her response. "Steve, I want you to do what God tells you to do. Whatever God tells you to do, I'll accept it."

Even to this day, I cherish those words. Despite her prayers and hopes for our marriage to be reunited, Patti was willing to truly trust God. Here was a woman who continued to love me despite all I had put her through and yet she was going to believe God no matter what He might tell me to do.

I began searching for a Biblical answer to the life dilemma facing me. My mother had an extensive library of Christian books and I spent the next week studying all references to the topics of divorce, separation, reconciliation, and marriage. Even though I found a lot of writings on these subjects, I was still uncertain how to apply the Bible's teachings within my own life circumstance.

Heeding my parent's suggestion, I sought the counsel of their pastor who helped me align my situation to what the Bible taught. He said to me, "Steve, you sinned by committing adultery and leaving your first wife, but God has forgiven you. However, you are now married to Camille and she has come to you wanting to be reconciled. You have a responsibility to honor those vows, Steve. You cannot unscramble the egg. You've already sinned, you've already been forgiven, and now you are in the state that you are in. The Bible talks about your situation in 1 Corinthians 7:24 when it says, 'So, dear brothers and sisters, whatever situation you were in when you became a believer, stay there in your new relationship with God.' According to what you have told me, Steve, you were married to Camille when you became a believer. Therefore, I would advise that you receive Camille back and do not get a divorce."

The pastor's counsel lined up with a lot of what I had been reading. I left his office and knew my answer. I could not unscramble the egg. I was married to Camille now and God was directing my path to remain faithful to her.

A week which had begun with my excitement to call Patti was now ending with my anguish to call her. My heart grieved. Once again I was going to abandon this woman. The phone call was understandably short.

"Hi, Patti. It's Steve."

"Hi, Steve." Her voice was quivering. "What have you decided?"

"This is hard Patti. I don't know how to...."

"It's okay Steve."

"No, Patti, it's not okay. I thought that God was bringing us back together just like you did and then all of this happened.

"What did you hear God saying?"

"Based on what I've read and what my parents' pastor told me, I should go back to Camille."

The wrenching silence on the other end of the phone was the sound of a broken heart. The depth of her faith revealed itself in her parting words.

"I understand, Steve. Go in peace. Go in peace."

Patti's release did allow me to go in peace. I drove to New Jersey and picked up my wife. As a reunited couple, Camille and I returned to the University of Tennessee at Chattanooga for my last semester before graduating with a degree in Economics. Of course, we had to find new housing, but other than that, I went back to my old routine of studying and working.

In the months prior to my going home for Christmas break, my job at the village mini market had actually provided a social outlet for me. The friendly bantering about my being an "old man" and "Jesus calling me here" resulted in the kids hanging around my cash register. Desiring to fit into their conversations, I unwittingly developed the art of storytelling. I wrapped humor and drama around the daily events in my life and turned them into entertaining escapades.

The stories were not about my life as you have read it, but rather about how God was helping me through the struggles of exams, exasperating professors, tight finances, lack of adequate sleep, and day to day life. The kids never knew about my pool playing history because pool was out of my life.

One evening, a student approached me with a request which would prove to be one of the first building blocks of God's ministry plan for my life. He said, "You know, Steve, I'm a Christian and I have been hanging around the store listening to your stories about how God has been working in your life. I'm wondering if you would come up to my dorm room after your shift and lead us in a Bible study?"

Without even considering the fact that I had never done this before, I responded, "Sure! I'd love to. See you around 12:30."

Yes, I meant 12:30 a.m. Dorm life was (and is) notorious for kids hanging out past midnight and not going to sleep until 2:00 or 3:00 o'clock in the morning. When I arrived to this young man's dorm room, four guys were waiting for me.

Since I did not know how to teach about God, my topic of conversation was simply to share about how God helped me get through life on a daily basis. I read the Bible regularly, keeping it always available among my textbooks. When I needed a break from my business books, I would turn to the Bible and inevitably a passage would apply to my life. These life applications were my topics of conversation and, amazingly, the guys wanted me to come back on a regular basis.

What I had not been doing on a regular basis was going to church. Every so often I would visit a local First Presbyterian Church college group, but I was never involved with Sunday services. Church just seemed to be a way to "act out one's religion" with God and I was more interested in "living out my relationship" with God.

My church opinion may have remained uncontested if it were not for a student I met through our Bible study. This young black man really had a heart for God. For the first time, my mind saw a possible connection between a love for the Lord and a person's involvement with church. Curious, I asked him, "What church do you go to?"

"I go to the Church of the First Born. Would you like to come and visit us on Sunday?"

"Sure. I'd like to."

He wrote down the address and on the next Sunday, I arrived at a "church." It did not look like a church. The storefront was deteriorated, with shattered windows and chipped paint. I questioned whether I was at the right place, but my ears were picking up the sound of music floating through the broken glass. I hesitantly walked inside.

The interior had the same condemned atmosphere as the exterior. The room was dingy, the chairs were broken, and the hymnals were shreds of paper struggling to hang on to their bindings. In addition, I was the only white person there. Everyone else in the congregation was black.

Obviously, I felt out of place, but I also remember feeling shocked. My church experience had always been in a church graced with glossy pews and beautifully bound hymnals. The presentation was pristine. These people were dressed up in their Sunday duds, but their surroundings were pathetic.

As I critically judged the scene in front of me and questioned why I was there, the Lord gently nudged my heart. "Steve, you wanted to come and see where that young man's faith was being nurtured. Well, you're here. Just sit down and pay attention." Obediently, I walked in and sat down in a rickety wooden chair.

No sooner had I settled in my seat when the pastor stopped speaking and said to me, "Welcome to the Church of the First Born. What's your name, Brother?"

Even though I was the one who had just walked in sticking out like a sore thumb, it took a moment before I realized he was speaking to me. Responding loud enough for the congregation of fifty to hear me, I answered, "My name is Steve."

Without batting an eye, the pastor then asked, "What does the Lord have for you to tell us today, Steve?"

I had just walked in! I came to receive a message, not to give a message! After being temporarily tongue tied, suddenly I realized that maybe I did have something to say. I told them the story about a young man within their congregation who sincerely loved God and how I had come to their church in search of the source which powered his faith.

Thus began my love affair with this congregation. I heard preaching, testimonies, and singing which penetrated my soul. Even though I had been reading the Bible faithfully since 1980 when Buddy Scallia told me, "It's in this Book, Steve. All of your answers are in this Book." I finally found my spiritual home. I found people who were living the Bible, who were depending on the Bible, and who treasured every word within the Bible. God was alive among these people and I was drawn into the folds of their church.

The pastor's name was Alfred E. Johnson. He worked in a foundry and had nine children with his wife Dorothy. He expounded the Word of God like I had never heard it before and his opening line before every sermon was "I just wanted you to know that I stopped by this morning on my way to heaven to let you know that Jesus never disappoints." One could almost sense that he really was "just stopping by on his way to heaven." He knew where his ultimate destination was and he was just stopping by to let you know the truth of what God had to say.

112

One day Pastor Johnson said, "Steve, I want you to come to the jail ministry with me and preach to the inmates."

"Pastor, I'm not a preacher!"

"Oh yes you are. You're a preacher."

"But I don't have any ordination."

"That's okay, Steve, you can still preach the Word of God."

"But I don't have any experience."

"This will give you experience."

"Okay, I'll go, but I don't want to preach."

"Steve, if you don't have the faith that you're a preacher, then I'll have the faith for you. I'll carry you if I need to carry you, but you're a preacher. Don't let anyone try to tell you otherwise."

I went with Pastor Johnson to the jail ministry and I did get up and preach. I have no idea what I said, but I remember men coming forward to receive Christ at the altar call afterwards. This was my second experience of people coming forward. My first experience had occurred just a few short weeks before my graduation.

Even though Camille had returned with me during my final semester, I continued to hold those late night Bible studies in the dorm after my shift at the village mini market. On one particular night, I ended our discussion by asking if anyone within our small group wanted to put their faith in God. We had apparently left the door open so that we were all surprised when we heard a voice from the hallway answer "I want to. I heard every word you said."

Unbeknownst to us, students had been sitting outside of the door listening! Immediately, this young man came walking through the door and prayed right then and there to receive Christ. Upon this young man's decision, I experienced a vision for ministry which I immediately shared with the group. "Maybe we should hold a more formal Bible study at the student center and ask the school to accredit it so that we can invite people from all over the campus to come." Everyone in the group agreed and the next day I filled out the appropriate club application.

Our Bible Study group was quickly approved and assigned a room at the student center. Our first "official" Bible study drew in almost ten students and within a few years after my graduation, it had grown to over one hundred in attendance. More precious to me than receiving my diploma was the honor of knowing that God had used me as His vessel to bring His Word to the University of Tennessee in Chattanooga.

CHAPTER 15

"Only simpletons believe everything they are told!
The prudent carefully consider their steps.
The wise are cautious and avoid danger;
fools plunge ahead with great confidence.
(Proverbs 14:15-16)

I was 35 years old when Camille told me the news. "Steve, we are going to have a baby."

We were going to be parents! I was going to be a father and we were going to be a family! Within months, our life was blessed by the birth of our beautiful daughter, Amanda.

Of course, a family has to be supported and after graduation I received a position as assistant manager at Crystal Corporation, a fast food restaurant chain based out of Chattanooga. Camille and I continued to be involved with the Church of the First Born. In fact she was just as excited about the pursuit of godliness as I was. I will always remember the day I came home from work and found the television had disappeared.

"Steve, I had to get rid of the TV."

"Why?"

"Because television was keeping me from the Lord. With the TV gone, I can listen to Christian radio and read the Bible more because I won't be tempted to watch my soap operas."

Our lives were finally united. We were in love with each other, we were in love with our new baby girl, Amanda, and we were in love with the Lord. Camille was involved with the women's ministry and I was still involved with the prison ministry as well as helping the pastor with many of the local church revivals. I was enjoying my role as a preacher.

Two years had passed and I was 37 when Camille once again told me the news. "Steve, we are going to have another baby!"

We were joyful. However, this pregnancy caused a change in Camille's temperament. She experienced uncontrollable fits of rage. I would come home from work and she would start yelling at me for no apparent reason. Eventually, her internal pendulum swung the other way and she would remorsefully cry, "Steve, I'm sorry. I don't know what happened to me. I don't know why I said all of those things."

Of course, anger and mood swings are just a few of the emotional side effects of pregnancy and, as a man, I did my best to cope. Unfortunately, Camille's fluctuating hormone levels did not stabilize after the birth of Sarah, our beautiful second daughter. Camille continued to verbally lash out at me and even though I tried to maintain my calm, the angry atmosphere within our household was beginning to wear on our relationship.

Attempting to fix whatever was causing Camille's anguish, I began to change our routine. Instead of attending the Church of the First Born where we had been actively involved, we began attending the First Presbyterian Church in downtown Chattanooga. Not only was this a transition from a black to a white church, but it was a black and white reversal of my church involvement. I missed preaching with Pastor Johnson! I was now just a pew sitter.

One Sunday while sitting in my pew, an invitation to go to the mission field was extended. A Coca Cola heiress had contributed sufficient funds to pay a year's expenses to France for anyone willing to travel there as a missionary. My soul stirred within me. Volunteering would not only allow me to get back into the ministry, but would also provide a sufficient income for our family to live on. I nudged Camille.

"This is perfect, Camille! This must be why we changed churches so that we could go into full time ministry. Let's go to France."

I then stood up, but I stood up alone. I looked back down at Camille and reached for her hand. She folded her arms and shook her head no. I sat back down on the edge of the pew facing her.

"Come on, Camille, stand up."

"No, Steve, I'm having enough trouble trying to make it here in the United States with two babies, and you want to drag me to France? I'm not going. If you want to go, you can go alone."

Right then I felt abandoned and angry. For the next week, I brewed about my inability to go to France. I even went to see the minister.

"Pastor, I stood up during the invitation last Sunday because I want to go to France. I feel that God is calling me and even though I am the head of the family, my wife is refusing to join me."

The pastor answered me wisely, but I did not like what he had to say.

"Steve, when God calls a family into ministry, He doesn't just call the husband, He calls the husband and the wife together."

Up until that incident, Camille had been the primary one between us to exhibit fits of rage. Now I was also angry and my lack of patience revealed itself in the acceleration of arguments between us. Not surprisingly, one day Camille said, "Steve, I'm going to take the babies and go to New Jersey to visit my family for six weeks. While I'm gone, maybe you can sort out what it is you want to do with your life because it's obvious you're not happy. You're frustrated and I'm frustrated."

Even though Camille left, the friction between us remained. In her absence I did not make any "life decisions." I wanted our marriage to work, but I was at a loss as to how to accomplish such a feat. Camille at least made an effort to fix our marriage because she took action by returning six weeks later with a list of "suggestions" regarding how our life should proceed.

Priority on the list was for us to either move back to New Jersey or for me to make more money. The financial stress of caring for two babies was apparently at the root of her discontent. I sensed our marriage was dependent on my willingness to comply. Having no desire to move back to New Jersey, I applied to Chick-fil-A®, a Christian owned fast food company.

After the typical interviews, I was offered an owner operator position which had earning potential into the six figures. I was thrilled until I opened the letter informing me of the store's location. It was in Woodbridge, New Jersey. I stared at those words and rebellion rose within me. Camille had wanted to "either" move to New Jersey "or" have me get a higher paying job. I had been willing to get a higher paying job, but I was not willing to let her have New Jersey too.

Trying to find an alternative career path which would lead away from New Jersey, I gave my current boss at Crystal Corporation the following ultimatum. "I've been offered an owner operator position at Chick-fil-A. Unless you can offer me a better management position with a higher salary, I will be giving my notice."

Much to my relief, the threat worked. My boss offered me more money along with a promotion to manage one of their stores in Albany, Georgia. I had been hoping to remain in Tennessee, but at least Albany, Georgia, was better than my submitting to Woodbridge, New Jersey.

Camille enthusiastically encouraged me to take the position. However, not knowing the underlying reason for my decline of the Chick-fil-A offer, she was unaware of my growing bitterness.

I worked hard at my new job which kept me away from home about sixty to seventy hours per week. My boss had apparently found his revenge for my threat because the store he assigned me had many problems similar to the Corner Pockets I had managed in Las Vegas. The job was stressful and my selfish reasons for accepting it were catching up to me. My aggravation was revealing itself in my dissatisfaction with life in general. Camille and I continued to bicker and our relationship frayed further. Camille began to badger me, "You know what? You're not happy with anything, Steve. Let's just get out of here. Forget the job and let's go back to New Jersey."

My short temper was not the only cause of our dissension, Camille bore her own share of the responsibility. However, Camille had an excuse. Unbeknownst to me until years later, Camille's bouts of depression and anger were triggered by a chemical imbalance developed during her pregnancy with Sarah. She never completely recovered from post partum depression and my self-centered nature fueled her negative reactions.

Tired of fighting both the work front and the home front, one day I came home from work particularly frustrated and I surrendered. "Camille, do you want to move to New Jersey?"

"Yes! I do."

"Okay. I'm quitting."

Little did I know that those simple words would soon spiral my life into forsaken loneliness. I gave my two week notice and we moved to New Jersey where I found a job as a bank auditor. My degree in economics was finally paying off until I tried to pay off an old bank debt.

I had been in my new position for about two months when my auditing team was assigned a bank where I had taken advantage of a bank error in the early 1970's during my drug days. Before the technology of computers, deposits and withdrawals were recorded manually by tellers who literally ink stamped the amount in a "passbook." I had gone into the bank one day to deposit $80, but the teller accidently stamped $800 into my passbook. At the time, I was a druggie, gambler, and hustler so that I had no qualms about taking advantage of this opportunity. I quickly closed my account, received my profit of $720, and walked out of the bank smiling.

The memory pricked my conscience. I was a Christian now and recalling what I had done created an overwhelming sense of guilt. My obligation was to make restitution. The money obviously had to be repaid.

When Camille learned of my plan, she was furious. "No! You can't do that! This affects me too and I didn't even know you back then. You have a wife and two babies to support and where are we going to get $720. We have no savings and you might even lose your job. Don't you dare tell them!"

Not responding well to dares, I countered, "I'm going to do it anyway. I'm going to confess."

Looking back, part of the reason I chose to confess was just to defy Camille. I blamed her for our unhappiness and I felt like I was the superior Christian and she should be following my lead. Whenever I detected her not going along with what I thought God's will was, I rebelled by choosing what she was against. Of course, I did not consciously think those thoughts, but obviously I was not grasping the basic concept of marriage.

119

Despite Camille's objections, the next day I went to my boss and explained, "Years ago I took advantage of a teller's $720 passbook error at the bank we are about to audit and I want to return the money."

"Steve, you can't do that. It's already been wiped off of the books. There's a seven year statute of limitations which has long passed. Forget it, Steve. You did it. You were young and you didn't know what you were doing."

"Do you have the authority to forget about it?"

"No, but do you really want me to go to my boss and tell him? It might cost you your job. Let's just drop it right here, Steve."

Seeing a great ministry opportunity, I began to tell him about my new desire to make amends for my past wrongs due to Jesus changing my life. He listened to me and then said, "Well, Steve, if that's what you want, I'll go to my boss, but I think you're making a big mistake."

Within 48 hours I was fired. When I told Camille, she was angry. Her screams and yells were the worst I had ever experienced. My defiant action ignited her chemical imbalance condition and she felt cheated, abandoned, deceived, and betrayed. Even her family turned against me and counseled her, "Steve's no good for you. He's not only hurting you mentally and emotionally, but he's abusing you with his religion."

Despite her family's advice to leave me, Camille hung on. The mooring of our marriage was not sunk ... yet.

Quickly, I found another lower paying job selling patio furniture at the same store where Camille would soon also work as an assistant manager of the Floral Department. Not quite learning my lesson, I told my potential new boss during the interview about my Christian beliefs. He said, "Well, Steve. I don't have a problem with your religion, but I don't want you to talk about Jesus on the job. I'm going to hire you, but if you talk about God on the job, you'll be fired."

After only one month on the job, I achieved top salesman status. And then this little old lady came into the store. I was her salesman and she was buying thousands of dollars worth of merchandise. She took a liking to me and at one point said, "I am having trouble in my life" and proceeded to share some personal struggles she was facing. Seeing my opportunity to witness, I began to share about my faith in Jesus.

My boss overheard and called me into his office immediately upon the woman's departure. "I told you not to talk about God on the job."

I defended myself. "But she wanted to talk about it and she was buying all of that merchandise. I had to continue to engage her in conversation to increase the sale! I'm already your top salesman and I've only been here a month."

"I don't care. You're fired."

Camille gave me an inquisitive look as she walked into the lunch room where I had loitered in order to tell her the news. At the time, my thoughts were only focused on the injustice of the situation. I should not have been fired. I was only talking about God. Now, as I write my story, my thoughts are focused on my selfishness to put my job at risk when Camille was working hard at not only holding down her own job in order to help us survive financially, but also using all of her remaining energy to raise and care for our two daughters.

"What are you doing here?" Camille asked. "It's not time for your lunch break."

"I got fired again."

"What did you do this time?"

"I talked to a customer about Jesus."

Needless to say I endured another outburst of choice words for my ignorance of the rules of employment while other employees listened in. Discouraged, I began my search for another job.

At the time, our new church was holding a pastor's conference. With my schedule suddenly freed up, I decided to slip in the back door to attend. I had enjoyed preaching with Pastor Johnson and I was still bitter about my missed opportunity to venture out as a missionary to France.

A well known Bible teacher was the keynote speaker via a simulcast from Atlanta. He said, "If God tells you to drive your car into a wall, then you drive your car into a wall. Our loyalty and obedience is the most important thing that we can offer Him."

As I listened, I was simultaneously conversing with God, "What do you want me to do Lord? I'll drive that car through a wall, I'll do whatever you want. I thought I was obeying you, but my marriage is in shambles. My life is a wreck. I've lost these jobs and I thought I was obeying you."

When the simulcast ended, an invitation was extended for those desiring to renew their commitment to God to walk forward and I did. Two pastors came up and knelt beside me. I learned later, too much later, that these pastors were visiting from another denomination which believed in some doctrines not directly aligned with the Bible. Their advice contradicted what I knew to be true, but I was grasping desperately for any "word from the Lord."

"Son, can we help you?"

I began to tell them about my marital problems, about my abandoning Patti, about my journey as a pool player, about my giving up pool, about earning my degree, about my enjoyment of preaching, about my desire to go into the mission field, about my job losses, about my current strained relationship with Camille, and about how my life was a complete mess. I shared with these two men my desire to be obedient to God's will for my life.

They listened, we prayed, and then they responded, "Son, you're living in an adulterous marriage and we've helped people in your situation. Your first wife was your true marriage. Your current wife is an adulterous marriage and you need to go home and tell your current wife that you made a mistake. You should leave her immediately, but you are to continue to pay support for her and your children. You are to never marry again and you are never to live with her in that adulterous marriage again. From this point on, you are to serve the Lord for the rest of your life as a single celibate man."

I went home and told Camille what these men had counseled. She stared wide-eyed at me and said with disbelieving words uttered barely above a whisper, "Are you going to believe that?"

Not at all grasping the serious fallacy of my reasoning, I responded, "I'm considering what they said. Maybe it's God's will which might explain why we can't get along."

Right before my eyes, Camille had a total and complete breakdown. She began to uncontrollably sob and she was riveted in emotional turmoil and pain. I watched my three year old

122

daughter, Amanda, crawl on top of her mother's lap trying to rescue her, crying, "Mommy! Mommy! It's okay Mommy. You're going to be alright. Mommy, stop crying."

The scene was a nightmare and I stood there lamenting to myself, "What have I done? What have I done to this woman? What have I done?"

Within a matter of days, I was served a restraining order which read, "This man is a threat to his wife and children and, in the best interest of the two children, Stephen Lillis will not be allowed to see, visit, or have any contact with his wife or children from this day forward." I was alone.

CHAPTER 16

"I am teaching you today - yes, you -
so you will trust in the Lord."
(Proverbs 22:19)

As if being served a restraining order was not enough, a knock on the front door sounded a short time later. Standing on the porch was Camille's cousin who also happened to be a local policeman. Armed with authority and determined to protect and serve, he commanded, "You've got twenty minutes to get your personal items and get off the premises. If you even come near Camille, I'll throw you in jail."

In twenty minutes I was on the street with the obvious question on my mind of "Where will I go?" I remembered a business card a man had given me at church the previous Sunday. We had been sharing about our personal lives and when he learned of my marital struggles he said, "Steve, I've been through a lot with my marriage. Because of a restraining order, my wife and children were taken away from me and I haven't seen them in thirteen years. Here is my card, call me if you need someone to talk to or if anything happens and you need a place to stay."

This man had no clue what was going to transpire in my life just one week later, but God knew and He had prearranged a place for me to go. I found a payphone and called the number on the card which was still in my jacket pocket.

"This is Steve. What happened to you has happened to me and I have no place to go."

"I understand. Here is my home address. I'll have food on the table and a room prepared. Stay as long as you need."

I stayed for about two weeks until I found a boarding house in Wyckoff, New Jersey. Ironically, this was the same city where I had met with Camille and her pastor at the Wyckoff Assembly of

God Church some four years earlier when Camille had asked for our marriage to be reconciled. The coincidence caused the clock of recollections to tick backwards. Had I made the wrong choice? I wanted time to tell me.

The day was my first Sunday at the boarding house and I was eating breakfast. My landlord, a kindly woman, asked, "Steve, would you like to join me and come visit my church this morning?"

"Sure, I'll go."

To my disbelief, she drove to my childhood hometown of Waldwick and pulled into the parking lot of the little brick schoolhouse which had housed kindergarten through eighth grade when I was a boy. I looked at her and said, "Is this your church? I went to school here as a boy."

"Yes, Steve. This is where we are starting a church. We are a group that came from the Wyckoff Assembly of God."

Without comprehending the personal significance of her last comment, my landlady calmly led the way to the church service which happened to be located in my old kindergarten room. My emotions were quickly fraying. My life had basically started in this room thirty four years ago and now this room was used to instruct the Word of God? Was the Lord trying to teach me something? What was going on?

The service began and the pastor asked, "Do we have any visitors here today?"

I raised my hand.

"Would you stand up and introduce yourself?

"My name is Steve Lillis."

"Are you any relation to Patti Lillis?"

My heart stopped, but my lungs burst forward, "Patti Lillis! She was my first wife! How do you know Patti Lillis?"

"I led her to the Lord seven years ago."

Bewilderment and wonder flowed through my soul. "You led Patti to the Lord? Do you know where she is? I would like to see her."

"Yes, we'll talk later."

After the pastor's answer, my mind was in a whirlwind of thoughts. I was here at a church which came from the church where the pastor had asked me to take Camille back as my wife and the pastor of this offshoot church knew the woman who had wanted to take me back as her husband. This was not adding up and yet here I sat in the same kindergarten room where I had learned how to add. God was certainly using irony to get my attention.

As the hour progressed, I regressed. I reminisced about my life as a five year old when my mother had brought me to this room for the first time. My fear of the unknown combined with my excitement to grow up and learn had me wanting to both grasp and release her hand simultaneously. I was afraid until my mother bent down and whispered, "Stephen, you're a big boy now and you're ready to learn new things. Everything is going to be okay."

Thirty four years later, I was sitting in the same room experiencing the same emotions of fear and excitement. Except this time instead of my mother bending down to reassure me, I heard my heavenly Father's voice saying, "Steve, I'm here. I understand your fears and I know you are uncertain about what the future holds, but everything is going to be okay. Trust Me."

Just as I had chosen to trust my mother, I inwardly chose to trust my heavenly Father. I was afraid of what the future held, but I was excited to enter God's classroom. With a new childlike faith, I prayed, "What do you want me to do, Lord? As usual, I'm messed up. I don't know why you are bringing Patti across my path again, but I will accept whatever you bring to pass. I'm here in my old kindergarten classroom, but it's literally your classroom now. I'm willing to start over and trust you. Please help me to listen and learn because I want you to be my teacher."

By the time the service had ended, I was a changed man. I did not know where my life journey would lead, but I knew God's path would lead me wisely.

True to his word, the pastor arranged a meeting with Patti at her home church, Calvary Temple Assembly of God in Wayne, New Jersey. The theme song "It's a Small World" was continuing to play itself in my life because Wayne had been the town our family had moved to when I was a teenager. My memory of those years of loneliness and rebelliousness resurfaced as I drove through the town's streets leading to the church. I had definitely made a lot of bad turns in life and they had only led to dead ends.

When I arrived at the church, Patti was standing near the front door conversing with someone. She saw me pull in the driveway and waved. That simple gesture put me at ease because I was nervous. Eleven years had passed since we had last seen each other and over four years had passed since we had last spoken. The hurt in her voice when I told her of my choice to reunite with Camille still resonated in my heart. I had no idea what to expect from this meeting, but I came hopeful.

I parked my car and as I walked toward the church, Patti reached for the hand of the man who she had been talking with. She was nervous too.

A moment of tentative silence elapsed when we finally came together as a group. Patti spoke first. "Hi, Steve. I want you to meet John. He has been my good friend for many years and now he is my husband."

I had not been prepared to meet Patti's husband. The pastor had left out this little tidbit of information, and I found myself needing to land on my feet quickly. A shock wave of disappointment had just blasted me while at the same time an emotional neutrality emerged because I knew what road my life would not be traveling down. Gaining my composure, I returned the introduction.

After some small talk, I asked John for permission to speak privately with Patti. I told him about my current marriage, about the restraining order, about going to church in my old kindergarten classroom, about meeting the pastor who had led Patti to the Lord, and about my belief that God orchestrated all of those events for a purpose. John listened and then looked to Patti who gave him a slight affirming nod. Protectively, John ushered us to the back of the church where Patti and I were able to sit and talk.

We talked for about three hours. I shared my failures and my sorrow for the hurt I had caused her. I repented and I confessed and she forgave me. We cried, we hugged, we shared, and we prayed. When we walked out of the sanctuary, John was waiting faithfully outside in the church lobby.

"Steve," he said, "I'm glad you came, but I don't want you to see Patti anymore. I don't want you to call her. I don't want you to talk with her. I don't want you to develop any relationship with her because she has spent years recovering from her painful past and I do not want you opening up her old wounds."

I respected his defense of the woman he loved and I humbly agreed to his demand. "No, John, I won't. I won't see her."

Upon gaining my agreement to his terms, he continued, "However, if you see her at a church meeting or if you run into her sometime, I'm going to accept that as the Lord's will and that God brought you together for an encounter. But I don't expect for you to cultivate any friendship or a relationship with Patti at any level. Understood?"

"I understand."

With nothing else left to be said, I hugged Patti good-bye and shook John's hand graciously. Patti had found a good husband who loved and cared for her.

Our paths never crossed again until about twelve years later. I was eating at a diner in Pompton Lakes, New Jersey, and I saw Patti walk in. She also spotted me and we looked at each other and smiled. We both remembered John's admonition that we were not to see each other or cultivate a relationship unless we ran into each other by Divine providence. God was allowing a chance meeting. Patti immediately came over and we shared for about forty-five minutes while she waited for her son to finish Karate lessons. It was a brief encounter, but one which comforted me with the knowledge that Patti was at peace.

CHAPTER 17

"Know the state of your flocks,
and put your heart into caring for your herds,
for riches don't last forever."
(Proverbs 27:23)

The restraining order was served to me on October 23, 1989, a date which has etched itself into my life's memory banks. During the days and weeks to follow, I literally cried myself to sleep every night. My family was gone and I was powerless to bring them back.

Camille's nervous breakdown had been medically diagnosed and the prescribed medications seemed to be helping her cope with the bouts of depression and anger. In fact, her emotions stabilized to the point where she dropped the restraining order after about three months. My girls were asking to see their daddy, and Camille softened. She even allowed me to move back in, but my stay lasted less than a week before I was kicked out again because I had lost another job.

Camille filled my absence with a boyfriend, but his addiction to drugs and alcohol only served to further my family's demise as he lured Camille back into the former lifestyle which we had escaped from together. The mixture of prescription and non-prescription drugs within her system reversed her short lived healing process and she once again spiraled into the behavioral effects of drug addiction. My fears about Camille's ability to care for our daughters haunted me as she increasingly exhibited emotional outbursts, depression, paranoia, and even some aggression.

I saw the girls once a week when I was allowed to take them to church. One Sunday when I stopped to pick up Amanda and Sarah, the boyfriend was sitting on the porch amidst a clutter of beer cans. While I was leaving with my daughters, he escorted me down the path and mockingly said, "If you want your wife back, renounce Jesus. Say that you don't believe in Him and you can have Camille back."

Even though my life flirted dangerously with hypocrisy, my faith was real. As much as I wanted Camille back, I would not yield to this man's temptation. I looked him in the eye and said, "Never. I will never renounce Jesus."

My response may have sounded righteous, but my spirit was humbly searching for God. I was a broken man and broke. I could not hold a job. Over the next couple of years I had too many jobs to count. My mind was not only distracted with my personal problems, but I also missed a lot of days in order to care for my girls due to Camille's drug induced irrational behavior. For example, while managing an A&W store one night, I received a call from Camille.

"Steve, you need to come right now and take the children, otherwise I'm going to kill them. I'm going to put them out in the snow and they are going to freeze to death."

Having no inclination to challenge Camille's dare, I left my job, picked up the girls, and cared for them until a week later when Camille called and said, "You need to bring the children back right now otherwise I'm going to call the police and tell them that you are violating visitation."

I not only lost this job, but many more like it. Camille harbored much hatred toward me and was not shy about communicating her vindictiveness. More than once she taunted, "Steve, I'm going to make it so that you can never hold a job. I'm going to ruin your life just like you've ruined mine."

The date was October 23, 1991, exactly two years to the day after receiving my first restraining order. Camille knocked on the door of my apartment and handed me a second restraining order. "Here, Steve. I want you out of my life and I don't want the children to see you anymore."

"Why?" I asked. She was high on something and her face exhibited bruising as if she had been beaten. "What's going on, Camille?"

She turned and walked away without answering. I opened the envelope and read the enclosed paperwork. I was being falsely accused of physical abuse.

My emotions surged with anger and fear. Anger because Camille was lying and fear because the relationship with my girls was legitimately threatened. How was I going to prove my innocence and convince the judge that I was a good father? A clue to my answer was found providentially the next morning. Even though my life was chaotic, I still read my Bible daily. My bookmark was in First Kings which contained a story about a mother who was trying to convince King Solomon to grant her custody of her child.

Two mothers who had lived together came to King Solomon in a custody dispute. Both had a son, but one of the sons had died in the night due to his mother accidently smothering him. When she woke up and discovered what had happened, she switched her dead baby with the other woman's live baby. When the other woman woke up and found her son dead, she wept. However, as the morning light grew, she saw that the boy was not hers.

The two women argued and their conflict was brought to King Solomon. After listening to their bickering, he ordered, "Both of you claim the living child is yours and both of you claim that the dead child belongs to the other. Bring me a sword. Now cut the living child in two and give half to each!" Then the woman who really was the mother of the living child cried out, "Oh no, my lord! Give her the child - please do not kill him!" The other mother said, "Go ahead, divide him between us. He will be neither yours nor mine."

Knowing now who the real mother was, King Solomon made his ruling. "Do not kill him, but give the baby to the woman who wants him to live, for she is his mother!"[16]

After reading this story, I argued with God. "You want me to release full custody to Camille and not fight the restraining order? But I didn't do anything wrong! I didn't beat Camille! If I let her do this without a fight, I might not ever get to see my girls again! God, I don't think I can do it."

However, the story kept nagging at me. King Solomon was able to see who truly loved the child by finding the mother who was

131

willing to give away her rights. Maybe the only way I could convey my innocence and love for my children was to surrender my rights for the sake of peace within our family. I prayed for God's wisdom.

Within a few days I found myself standing in front of a judge answering to charges of assault.

"Stephen Lillis, did you physically assault your wife?"

"No, your Honor, I did not."

"Camille Lillis, did your husband physically assault you?"

"Yes, he did and I don't want him to see me or the children anymore."

The judge looked back and forth between the two of us. Camille appeared disheveled and obviously drug ridden. With a trace of understanding, the judge addressed me.

"What do you want, Mr. Lillis?"

"Your Honor, whatever my wife wants, let her have it."

"Do you realize that you have rights here?"

The judge was trying to help me. Was I going to accept his subtle offer and fight for my rights? After all, I had done nothing wrong. Or had I? Of course I had never physically abused Camille, but memories of my selfish motives and actions within our marriage surfaced. I had always fought for my way and had done what I wanted. Rarely had I considered Camille's input or advice. She was obviously wrong in what she was doing, but she was fighting for what she felt was right.

I looked across the aisle at Camille. Suddenly, she did not appear as my accuser, but rather as a picture of my failure as a husband. She just wanted the same thing as me. A family. My heart softened and I sensed God's reassurance. "Give your family to me. Surrender all of your rights and let Camille have what she wants. Allow me to heal your family."

King Solomon's story played again in my mind. Love had motivated the mother of the living child to give up her rights. I chose to allow my love for Camille and my girls to motivate my response to the judge.

"Your Honor, in the interest of peace, I want my wife to have what she wants."

Obviously surprised by the turn our case was taking and in an attempt to sway Camille, the judge addressed her.

"Mrs. Lillis. Are you sure this is what you want?"

"Yes, I don't want him to see me or the children."

The restraining order stood and I left the courtroom not knowing if I would ever see my family again. King Solomon had immediately reunited the mother and son in the story, but I did not know if or when God would allow me to be reunited with Camille or my children.

Worry continued to envelop my mind over the next months. How were my children? How was Camille treating them? Would I ever get to see them again or would I be like the man who had not seen his family for thirteen years? Why could I not hold a job? Even though Camille's interruptions to my jobs had stopped, I still kept getting fired. Apparently, the problem was me. I had always depended on myself, but God was apparently teaching me to be dependent on Him because I did not get a good job until I gave up and prayed, "What do you want me to do, Lord? I can't take this anymore. I go to work and I get fired. You are going to have to bring a job to me."

He did. Ironically, God landed me a position at a location which I had rejected years earlier. Humor is definitely one of His characteristics.

The deacon at my church had invited me over for dinner and afterwards we had gone down to the basement. Without coming down the stairs, his wife symbolically called down to us from above, "Hey, Steve, I just saw in the paper that they are looking for a manager at the Chick-fil-A in Woodbridge."

When I heard her say "Chick-fil-A in Woodbridge," I knew it was God. The Chick-fil-A in Woodbridge was the same store where I had refused to go five years earlier when Camille had given me the ultimatum of "either find a higher paying job or move back to New Jersey." If I had not stubbornly turned down the offer, I would have been the owner operator of this exact store.

The next day I nervously applied for the job. The circumstances smacked of God's involvement, but my deflated self image held little hope of being hired. Despite my discouragement, I sensed

God saying, "Steve, just be who you are. Be honest. Just do the interview and I will take care of you."

Tom Walsh, the owner, conducted the interview. "Well, Steve, what makes you want this job and why are you here?"

I began to tell him my story about how I had turned down the offer of his Chick-fil-A store five years earlier. I shared my marital situation and confessed my inability to hold a job. My life story unfolded during the course of a long interview. At the end, Tom said, "Steve, you're hired. I believe you and I believe God has His hand on your life and I want to be a part of whatever God has planned for you."

Disbelieving my ears, but believing within my heart, I started work at the Chick-fil-A in Woodbridge. Even though most of my work experience was in the fast food industry, the job was not easy. The environment was fast paced and volatile due to lunch and dinner food rushes. Customers came, the cashier lines backed up, and the cooks had to prepare the orders quickly. As the manager, I had to fill in wherever I was needed, and I cracked under the stress. My emotional pressure outside of the job prevented me from handling the pressure inside of the job.

Employees began to complain to my boss. "He's like a dictator. He yells at us to go faster and we're going as fast as we can. He can't handle a lot of orders at once and then takes it out on us. He gets frustrated, but he's the one not doing his job!"

The handwriting was on the wall. Even my God given job was going to be short-lived. These were not new complaints and I had been fired for similar reasons many times before. The day arrived. It was the middle of a busy rush and I was rudely barking at the employees to work harder and faster. Tom, the owner, walked in and, after observing the chaos, called me to the back for what I knew was the inevitable. He had caught me in the act of mismanagement.

"Steve, how would you like to come join me for lunch. Let's go get a steak and lobster. My treat."

I stared back at Tom in disbelief.

"What! I figured you called me back here to fire me. We're in the middle of a lunch rush and if you're not firing me then I've got to get back! We're swamped!"

"Steve. Money is not important. You are. Come on, Steve, I want to take you out to lunch. Don't worry about the business. It will take care of itself. God will watch it."

Unbelievably, he took me out to lunch at a fancy seafood restaurant. He talked with me and entered into my pain. He listened to my concerns about my children and my wife and then he took me back to work.

A few weeks later, Tom again came to the store during a food rush and found me cracking under the pressure. Once again, he called me to the back.

"Yeah, Tom, I know. I'm messing up again."

"Steve, I'm hungry. What would you like to eat today? Steak? Lobster? Italian? Let's go get lunch."

"But Tom, we're in the middle of the lunch rush. I'll do better. Let me get back to work."

"Steve, don't worry about the business. You're more important than the business."

Tom took me to another nice restaurant and he shared in my pain as I talked about my shambled life. Over the next six months, Tom continued this routine with me until I finally broke under the pressure of love. I was not deserving of the mercy being extended to me. For the first time, I wanted to change my behavior not because of my own self-serving ambitions, but rather to express gratitude and service to someone else. My heart opened up to the possibility of seeking help.

CHAPTER 18

"Every word of God proves true.
He defends all who come to Him for protection."
(Proverbs 30:5)

Not having a television, I listened to the radio a lot. One station frequently ran an advertisement for a Christian therapy clinic located in California.

> Our service is dedicated to helping you achieve greater emotional and spiritual health. Within a Christian atmosphere of warmth and caring, we guide you in developing new approaches for dealing with old problems. We can help. Call us today.

I often wondered if I could get Camille to attend counseling. After all, she needed help. However, the past months of experiencing Tom's unwarranted kindness brought my own shortcomings to light. Maybe I was really the one who needed treatment.

With a new willingness to change myself, I asked Tom for time off in order to seek professional guidance. Not surprisingly, he said, "Go ahead, Steve. You are more important than the business. Your job will be here for you when you get back."

Tom drove me to the airport and I flew to California. The Christian therapy clinic was actually within the psychiatric wing of a hospital so that I was required to sign myself in. The road to my mental health included private counseling with doctors as well as a requirement to participate in group sessions. As I listened to the life stories of other patients, my own problems paled in comparison.

One distraught girl shared an experience from childhood. Her mother had driven their car to a park, said good-bye, and then walked away from the car never to return again. The memory of literally watching her mother's desertion had caused severe mental and emotional trauma within this girl's life.

Listening to her story and many others like it, I thought, "Wow. I don't have those kinds of memories. I had a wonderful mother and father. No one ever did me wrong. I had a good life. All of my problems are because of what I've done, not because of what others have done to me."

Silently I prayed, "What do you want me to do, Lord? My problems are nothing compared to these peoples' problems, but I still need healing from what is going on in my life. Will you help me?"

His help came the next day while I was reading the Bible. Our in-patient regimen also prescribed structured private time and amidst the quiet meditation of my heart, my soul heard God's reprimanding counsel.

"Steve, when will you believe me? You have traveled three thousand miles to California and I am going to tell you the same thing here that I have told you before. Every word in the Book you hold in your lap is true. I will never leave you nor forsake you. I will never put more on you than you can handle. I will work all things together for good to those who love me. And Steve, I know you love me, but will you trust me? Everything you have read for the past ten years since I introduced you to the little shoemaker who shared Ephesians 6:12 with you is true. I have given you truth, but you must personally answer the question. Do you believe what I've told you in my Word? Because if you do believe, then you can sign yourself out of this hospital and go home. But if you don't believe, then you are going to end up like many people here trying to find solutions other than what I have already provided."

God's question loomed in my heart. Did I believe? I looked at the Bible in front of me. To believe or not to believe? The choice was mine and I made my decision.

Yes, I believed. The moment I committed to those words, I experienced restoration. I was going to be okay. I held the key to my complete healing in my hands. The Word of God. The Bible. Just like the little shoemaker, Buddy Scallia, had told me, "You will get all of the answers to all of your questions if you will put your faith in what this Book says. It's in this Book, Steve. All of your answers are in this Book. Jesus Christ is the Lord of the universe and He has allowed these events in your life so that you will choose to place your faith in Him."

For many years I had "professed" faith in God, but I had not "placed" my faith in Him. I was like a man looking at a chair. He could believe the chair legs would support him if he chose to sit down, but his belief would not be exercised until he actually sat in the chair. I smiled as I remembered a verse from Deuteronomy 33:27.

"The eternal God is your refuge,
and His everlasting arms are under you."

Those chair legs were like God's arms. More than just believing, He wanted me to exercise my faith by choosing to actually place the weight of my burdens into His everlasting arms. God was my refuge and my only true protection. Since adolescence, I had entrusted my life to other things like sports, pool, money, and personal ambition, but these shaky supports had collapsed and failed. With the eyes of my heart now opened, I understood. No life trauma or suffering could destroy me when I took refuge in the eternal God. Because God was my refuge, I could dare to be bold.

I signed myself out of the hospital and I have not doubted God in that kind of way again. My life experienced new growth. Two years earlier I had been in God's kindergarten classroom and now I felt like I had graduated from grammar school. However, high school loomed ahead.

Tom welcomed back not only a new man, but a new manager. I no longer cast blame for my problems at others. Instead, I remained focused on the task at hand and how I could cooperate with my employees. Our Chick-fil-A was soon awarded the distinction of being one of the top ten franchises out of five hundred restaurants. Tom and I were making beautiful restaurant music together.

The silence from my family was still deafening, however. I had not seen Camille or the girls since my judicial hearing seven months earlier. The law allowed for a review every six months and I requested a court date for the purpose of seeking permission to visit my children.

On the day of court, Camille sat on one side and I sat on the other. The judge asked us to come forward.

"What are you two doing here again? I thought we resolved this matter the last time?"

"Your Honor," I said, "I wanted to ask my wife a question and I wanted to do it legally. The only way I could talk with her was to appear back in this courtroom. May I speak with her?"

The judge looked to Camille who shrugged her shoulders and nodded affirmatively.

"You've got five minutes. Bailiff, escort them to my chambers."

Humbly, I spoke to Camille. "Sweetheart, I'm so sorry for what I've done to you and I want you to know I'm only here for the sake of our children. I would like your permission to see the girls on whatever terms you want. I'm going to keep my word and if you don't want me to see them, I won't. I'm just here to ask your permission."

Camille looked at me curiously. I was out of character. My typical demeanor of authoritarianism was tamed.

"Well, the girls have been asking for you, but I don't want to see you. I don't want to have anything to do with you!"

"That's okay sweetheart, I'll do whatever. A court ordered visitation with court supervision is fine. Whatever you want. I'm only here to ask your permission and whatever you say goes."

The bailiff knocked gently on the door letting us know our five minutes were up. We walked back to the courtroom and sat down once again on our separate sides. While we waited our turn, other domestic cases were presented to the judge. In each case, the couples were spewing hate at one another. They were fighting over the children, over the money, and over anything that they thought the other person might want. Anger and revenge filled the room. It was ugly.

I glanced over at Camille and found her looking at me. She gave me a slight nod as if to say, "Come here." I verified by pointing at myself and then at her and she nodded her head "yes." I waited for an appropriate time within the court proceedings and then I walked to the other side and sat down next to Camille.

"Yes, sweetheart, did you have something else?"

"Steve. Isn't this horrible what we're hearing? Everyone hates each other."

"Yeah. It's sad."

"You know what? I don't want to be like them. I'm going to drop all of the charges. We don't have to do court supervision. We're going to get out of here. I trust you now, Steve."

The judge, noticing my movement in the courtroom and seeing additional conversation going on beyond our allotted five minutes, expedited our case on the docket.

"Mr. and Mrs. Lillis. Come forward. What agreement have you come to?"

Camille spoke first. "Your Honor, I'd like to drop all of the charges. We are going to take care of this outside of the court-room."

The judge cast an accusing glance at me and then interrogated Camille.

"Did he threaten you just now and in that back room?"

"No. He didn't threaten me. He was very nice and under-standing."

"Well, listen, young lady. You have been in and out of this courtroom for the past two years and you have had our help. If you leave now, you will not have the assistance of this court anymore."

"That's okay, because I don't want it anymore."

"Fine. See the bailiff to sign the papers. Case closed."

The knock of the gavel sounded against its hardwood core and the softening of Camille's hard heart knocked against the core of my being. I had not even said a word! What had God done? I had only hoped for a court ordered supervision and now the court was not even involved.

We signed the papers and walked out. Camille once again spoke first.

"Steve, I want you to come see the children this Sunday and take them to church again."

140

"Whatever you want, sweetheart."

Since that day in court, not only have we never been back, but we have never spoken hostile words to each other again. Shortly after returning from California, a wise pastor had counseled me from 1 Peter 3:7 regarding my role as a husband.

> In the same way, you husbands must give honor to your wives. Treat her with understanding as you live together. She may be weaker than you are, but she is your equal partner in God's gift of new life. If you don't treat her as you should, your prayers will not be heard.

Even though we were not living together, Camille was my wife and when I began to treat her with kindness and understanding, my prayers were being heard. God was healing my relationship with my family.

The relationship with my boss and career was also going smoothly. The year was 1993 and I had maintained a steady job while at the same time earning several managerial awards for almost three years. Tom had frequently called me into his office where he had surprised me with bonuses based on the performance ratings we were receiving. One day he called me into his office and really surprised me.

"Steve, it's time for you to leave Chick-fil-A."

"What!" My tone of shock was undisguised.

"No, no, no. Don't misunderstand me, I'm not firing you. I just know you can do more with your life than work as a restaurant manager. God has given you a healing and I've done my job with you. Now it's time for you to move on and do bigger things for Him."

I remained silent until I could find my voice.

"Tom, how can you do this? There's still a lot of money to be made!"

"No, Steve. You're more important than money which is what I have been trying to tell you. I'm going to lose a good manager, but the Kingdom of God is going to benefit from your service elsewhere and that is what is most important. So, Steve, where do you want to go? What do you want to do with your life? I'm here to help you."

Tom did not immediately send me out to the streets. For weeks after our meeting, he spent many hours studying Scripture with me. We prayed together, petitioning God to reconcile my marriage with Camille and to guide my future decisions. Tom asked questions about what I liked and what I did not like. I specifically remember the point in one of our conversations when I said, "Well, I've always wanted to be a teacher."

CHAPTER 19

"Timely advice is as lovely as
golden apples in a silver basket."
(Proverbs 25:11)

Tom helped me look for my first teaching position. Because I already had a college degree, I could get my teaching certification if I was hired as a trainee for one year. I found a director named Dr. Frederick H. Laguarde of an Afrocentric school in Paterson, New Jersey, who was willing to hire me for a two year contract. The first year allowed me to earn my certification and the second year allowed me to return the favor.

Even though I was the only white instructor of a curriculum which taught black culture and history, I fit in. God had prepared me for this job many years earlier when I worked with Pastor Johnson at the Church of the First Born. The bond I had developed with my prior black congregation carried forward with a love for my new co-workers and students.

A teacher's salary was always disreputably low, but my salary was even lower than low because of my lacking a resume. As a result, I lived in missionary housing and also took a job as an after school program director at an inner city church in Paterson, New Jersey. God used this part time position to spark a change in my perspective about pool.

Since I had laid down my cue stick nine years earlier, I had not revisited the sport. Even Tom had tried to sway me to play again "for the Lord," but I had resisted his suggestion. The pastor at the inner city church was the one who began to break through my barriers. He came to me one day with a request.

"Steve, our youth group wants to do some street evangelism at the local pool room. We've heard about your pool playing and we want you to come along and do a demonstration in order to arouse some interest in the crowd. You won't have to say anything. Just do some trick shots and the kids will do the talking. Will you help us out?"

Unable to come up with a viable excuse, I hesitantly agreed. On the day of the event, I stepped up to the pool table and performed some trick shots. True to the plan, people gathered around and the kids began to mingle among the pool players, even praying with some of them! After the event was over, I pondered the question of whether pool could actually be used for some godly good, but I made no effort to contemplate the answer.

However, I did have to answer Camille's request for more child support money. I had not been able to afford much on my pittance of a salary and I knew her request was valid because our girls were growing up. They were in elementary school now.

With my two year contract at the Afrocentric school fulfilled, I applied within the public school system and was offered a position which paid triple the salary. In addition, I took a part time job as a school bus driver. The increased income helped me to give more money to Camille and raise my own standard of living. I even began pursuing a master's degree. My life was finally experiencing a semblance of peace.

Even the relationship with my parents was renewed. After retirement, they became missionaries with "SOWERS - Servants On Wheels Ever Ready." Traveling via motor home, they offered volunteer assistance in repair, construction, and maintenance work to needy Christian ministries such as churches, schools, colleges, camps, and retreats. Whenever they had an assignment within driving distance, we made plans to see each other.

During the summer of 1995, my parents were nearby in Hershey, Pennsylvania, and I drove out to visit them for the weekend. As I dressed for church on Sunday morning, my mother requested a change of plans.

"Stephen, rather than go to church this morning, there is something I'd like for you to see here at the campground."

"What is it, Mom?"

"It's a Gospel magician and he's doing a show in the club house."

"A Gospel magician? That doesn't even sound right! I think I'd rather go to church."

As a boy, I had been the one trying to wiggle out of going to church and now she was the one wiggling. Our roles had reversed, but I will never forget her next words.

"Son, you've got to take God out of the box. Open your mind and allow Him some creativity. God is not constrained to a church building, Stephen. Trust me, if you go, you will not be disappointed."

Even though I remained unconvinced, I agreed to go. On the walk over with my parents, my mother continued to prime me.

"Most of the campgrounds we stay at offer Sunday morning services and usually only about five to ten people attend. But, Stephen, pay attention to how many families are going to show up on a Sunday morning to hear about the Bible just because a magician is here."

She was right. We walked into the club house and over a hundred people had already filled the chairs. We found a seat. Intrigued, I studied the stage set before me filled with a variety of standard props used by the typical magician. How was he going to weave the Bible into traditional magic?

The audience ranged from toddlers to seniors and everyone clapped when Mr. Bracilano, a gray haired man in his early sixties, stepped onto the stage and announced, "Welcome to today's magic show, 'Creation to Christ.'"

Throughout the next hour, I sat spellbound as I watched familiar Bible stories being told through the art of magic. Plants and animals were popping out of things to represent Creation. Water turned into blood (or something red) as he told the story of Moses, the Nile River, the ten plagues and the parting of the Red Sea. When he finished with the account of Jesus' death and resurrection, an altar call was given and about fifteen people raised their hands.

As I sat in amazement at what I was witnessing, I felt my mother's elbow poking me in the side.

"See! God is not restricted."

She was right. I was fascinated. My mind was pinballing with possibilities. After the show, I walked up and waited my turn to talk with this man who was creatively using his magician talents to spread the Gospel.

"Mr. Bracilano," I exclaimed, "that was amazing! Do you think I could do what you do with billiards instead of magic? I'm not a magician, but I was once a top pool player and I traveled the country with Mike Massey, the greatest trick shot artist ever. I've got a hundred trick shots up my sleeve that I can perform on a pool table. Do you think there is any way I can use my tricks on a pool table to share the Gospel like you just did with your magic tricks?"

I will never forget his answer. He placed his hand on my shoulder and in a deep godly booming voice said, *"Son, not only can you do it, but you must!"*

It was like I had heard the voice of God. I walked away in wonder. For the next five months, I could not get his booming voice out of my mind, *"Son, not only can you do it, but you must!"* I even called him one time in order to ask more questions and he once again delivered the same exhortation, *"Son, not only can you do it, but you must!"*

I wrestled with God on the subject. My life history was not a good resume for becoming a missionary. In addition, just like I had not initially seen the connection between magic and the Gospel, I knew the combination of the Bible and billiards would evoke skepticism within others.

Many people do not view the game of pool as a wholesome activity. More often than not, when asked to think of a billiard scene, people render an image of a group of cigar smoking bulldogs hovering around a pool table with beer in their paws and money on the table. The only image sometimes left out is Fifi, the gorgeous French white poodle!

No, intertwining the message of the Gospel with pool would not be an easy task. The patrons in billiard environments are typically not receptive to hearing about God and pool hall managers are hesitant to allow someone to publicly tell their gambling, carousing, and drinking customers about a God who may lead them away from the owner's profitable venture. With mutual dubiousness, the church is also hesitant to associate with an activity traditionally tied to such worldly business establishments. How could I be a friend to both worlds when both worlds were at odds with each other?

146

I presented the question to some men within my church at Hawthorne Gospel. They immediately grasped the dichotomy and yet open mindedly counseled, "Steve, given your pool background, maybe God does want you to use billiards to preach the Good News of the Gospel of Jesus Christ." Even with their encouragement, the division in my mind still existed. I continued to avoid God's still small voice until He forced me to listen.

The invitation came from my church friend, Ken Resztak. "Steve, come over to my house this Friday and you can give me some lessons on my new pool table. I know you have been struggling with whether God might be calling you to use your billiard skills within the ministry and we can spend some time talking about it."

Little did I know that the night of the invitation would be the opening debut of the historic "Blizzard of '96.'" On January 6, 1996, an incredibly massive storm hit the entire Eastern seaboard. Snowfall records were widespread including 24.9 inches in Roanoke, Virginia; 30.7 inches in Philadelphia, Pennsylvania; and 27.8 inches in Newark, New Jersey.[17]

And where was I stranded for three days while this powerful storm crippled government, commerce, and travel? I was left standing at a pool table in the basement of another man's home. The irony of God had struck again.

Taking his unexpected house guest in stride, Ken said, "Well, Steve, God has apparently given us this time here at the pool table. Since you've already shown me the basics, teach me one of your easy trick shots."

I chose a few simple tricks to teach Ken and then, at his urging, I began to demonstrate many of my more complex shots. After watching one particular stroke where I had sent a ball between two rows of balls, Ken said, "These are all really good! I think there is a way you can use them to share the Gospel. That last shot could be called *The Parting of the Red Sea.*" My own soul almost parted upon hearing his words. The Gospel magician had performed a trick about this famous Bible event and the memory caused his booming godly voice to sound off once again, ***"Son, not only can you do it, but you must!"***

147

The storm clouds may have been squalling on the outside, but the "*Son*" was suddenly shining on my inside. I finally understood how God could use billiards to share the Gospel message of Jesus. With new found purpose, Ken and I enthusiastically identified Biblical perspectives and life lessons for each trick shot. By the time roads were cleared for travel, we had a script prepared for a Gospel trick shot show. Mr. Bracilano's affirmation that it could be done was proven true, but whether I would do it or not was yet to be determined.

The secret of what we had done was safe with me. I made no effort to tell my church or advertise our newfound show. Instead, I simply (or dangerously) prayed, "God, if you want me to move forward with this, you're going to have to do something miraculous to show me."

Three days later, I received a phone call from Tom, my old boss at Chick-fil-A. We had not spoken to each other in almost three years since he had helped me find my first teaching job at the Afrocentric school.

"Hi, Steve, I know it's been awhile and I don't know what you're up to these days, but I'm calling to ask you a big favor. You see, one of our deacons just got a new pool table in his basement. He wants to minister with it and has invited the youth group to his home next weekend. I told him that I knew this former professional pool player who could do some amazing trick shots and he was hoping you would come and do a demonstration for the kids."

Why were basements and pool tables suddenly popping into my life? Tom continued, "Now I know you're hesitant to involve yourself with pool, but would you please come and do a couple of shots?"

God could not have used a lightning bolt to get my attention any more than He just had. With a feeling of calm after the storm, I answered, "Tom, your phone call is a direct intervention from God." I told Tom about my being trapped in a basement during the storm with only a pool table and a church friend who pushed me to write a script full of Scriptural lessons using my various trick shots.

148

Even though I accepted Tom's invitation, I still wanted further confirmation. In the Bible's New Testament, missionaries were always sent out by the church. If my calling was from God, then I needed to be held accountable by a body of believers. My church, Hawthorne Gospel, would have to send me.

I laughed at God internally. "You may have been able to maneuver getting me back at the pool table and you may have been able to get me to consider playing pool for you, but we both know that it's the rare church which would endorse a pool playing missionary. I don't see a chance in heaven for the church to send me. My past is not only marred with gambling and drugs, but I'm separated from my wife and family. There's no way you will be able to convince a church to use me. But I'm willing to see what you can do. I'll go to the Wednesday prayer meeting and, during the meeting, I'll ask for prayer to send me out as a pool playing missionary.

The prayer meeting's itinerary typically included a short sermon. When the Associate Pastor, Howie Van Dyk, announced the title of his message: "The Lord can use whatever gift or talent you have to offer," I smiled. God was obviously having a good laugh at my expense.

Pastor Howie knew me, but he did not know much about me. Back when Camille and I were trying to make our marriage work, we had scheduled a counseling appointment at the church. We just "happened to be" Pastor Howie's first couple to counsel on his first day of serving at Hawthorne Gospel Church. As a result of that counseling session, he did know I was a pool player with a speckled past. That information was apparently enough for him to use me as an impromptu illustration.

"Take Steve here," Pastor Howie walked over and laid his hand on my shoulder, "he used to be a professional pool player and I believe that even Steve Lillis can use his pool talents to serve God somehow, someway."

My heart was in my throat. Pastor Howie was clueless as to what was going on in my life. He did not know about Ken, the script, Tom's invitation, and my desire to be sent. He knew nothing! The hairs on my arms stood up and the back of my neck tingled as I interrupted his talk.

"Excuse me, Pastor Howie. You don't know this, but in two days I'm going to perform a Gospel trick shot show for a youth group and I came here tonight to ask for the church to send me out in prayer."

Without a moment's hesitation, Pastor Howie said, "Well, let's pray right now."

Three days later, on January 20, 1996, I did my first Gospel trick shot show for Tom Walsh and his church's youth group. After watching my presentation, Tom came up to me and said, "Steve, this is going to be used around the world. I believe the Lord is ordaining a pool ministry."

At that moment, I willingly rendered my pool playing talents to God. Gospel Trick Shot was born.

CHAPTER 20

"I will teach you wisdom's ways
and lead you in straight paths. "
(Proverbs 4:11)

My life transitioned over the next few months. I completed my Masters in Education with a concentration in Administration and Supervision from St. Peters College in Jersey City. I even had the paperwork prepared for my pursuit of a PhD at Seton Hall University, but I laid it aside because my focus had changed. My new desire was to teach others about God and I eagerly wanted to nurture my newborn ministry.

Having only one event in my repertoire to build upon, I began asking pool rooms and churches if I could do a Gospel Trick Shot show in an effort to find more audiences. I was able to schedule a few performances, but they were not enough to satisfy my thirst for more.

Since God had been the one who turned my heart back to pool, I petitioned Him for guidance. "Lord, you obviously gave me this desire to use my talent for your glory, but where am I to go? What do you want me to do?"

My prayer stopped short as I uttered those last words. Scenes from my life flashed across the screens of my memory as I recalled asking God the same question over and over again.

When I had contemplated suicide and saw the light on the ceiling, I asked, *"What do you want me to do, Lord?"* He led me to join the Navy.

When I was praying in the Las Vegas Tropicana hotel room and experienced another vision of light, I implored, *"What do you want me to do, Lord?"* He led me to Mike Massey and Chattanooga.

When I laid down my cue stick after Camille left me, I cried, *"What do you want me to do, Lord?"* He led me to the University of Tennessee.

When I had restored my relationship with Patti and Camille requested restoration of our marriage, I questioned, *"What do you want me to do, Lord?"* He led me back to Camille and gave me two beautiful daughters.

When I quit my Albany job in Georgia and then lost my bank and patio furniture jobs in New Jersey, I beseeched, *"What do you want me to do, Lord?"* He led me faithfully through the heartache of being separated from Camille and my daughters.

When I humbly sat in a church which used to be my kindergarten classroom as a boy, I entreated, *"What do you want me to do, Lord?"* He led me to Tom Walsh at Chick-fil-A.

When I signed myself in to the Christian Therapy Clinic, I probed, *"What do you want me to do, Lord?"* He led me to become a teacher.

At every turn in my life, I had asked God the same question and hindsight revealed His answer. He had led me. Despite all of my failures and poor decisions, God had faithfully led me on a life journey leading to a closer walk with Him.

I understood. God simply wanted me to trust Him. He did not want me to "do" something, He wanted me to "be" someone who believed and had faith in His Word. God did not want religion from me, He wanted a relationship with me. Responding to His gracious mercies, my soul willingly yielded itself into God's everlasting arms. Never again would I ask the question, "What do you want me to do, Lord?" Instead, I would ask the more relevant question, "Lord, how can you use me?"

The greatest worship I could offer God was presenting my life to be used as His willing vessel. I did not know how He would use me because I had a self-serving personality, a sinful past, and I was separated from my wife, but I was finally ready to rely on the answer He had been giving me for so many years. "Trust Me."

My dad would soon pass away, but he would literally spend the last year and a half of his life helping my ministry get started. Since he had given me my pool table as a boy, I am sure he questioned the fatherly wisdom of his action many times. Pool had been the vehicle which had led me down many wrong paths in life and yet my dad had encouraged me to perfect my skills. Watching me abuse my ability must have broken his heart, but now seeing my desire to use my talent to serve the Lord would act as a healing balm reaching into the depths of both of our souls. My heavenly Father was going to allow my earthly father to die peacefully knowing that his wayward son had returned.

As if God was giving me a second chance at childhood, He jumpstarted my ministry under the leadership and guidance of my parents. As missionaries with SOWERS, my dad and mom spent their time at churches, schools, camps, retreats, and RV parks which were all prime candidates for welcoming Gospel Trick Shot shows. They would call me almost every week, "We're up in New York, can you come up here?" Or, "We're over here in Pennsylvania and they want you to do a show." Without any plan except for the script written during the blizzard and my newfound trust, I hopped from location to location. My parents moonlighted as booking agents as they filled my calendar every week.

My audiences had the expectation of hearing a Biblical message unlike the few shows which I had performed in pool hall environments where hecklers abounded. In His wisdom, God nurtured my boldness and confidence within the environment of venues which were not ideologically opposed to either pool or religion. The onlookers were predominately non-pool players and their curiosity about the billiard related delivery of the Gospel superseded the natural inclination to perceive me as a threat.

An element of showmanship was required in order for my performances to be successful. Just like the magician had drawn the audience into his tricks, I had to allure the spectators with a semblance of drama and entertainment. My role model was someone who I had met early on in my pool career. His name was

153

Rudolf Wanderone, better known for his impersonation of Minnesota Fats from "The Hustler" movie.

The year was 1983 and I was in Tupelo, Mississippi, playing in a professional 9-Ball tournament. Minnesota Fats, affectionately known as "Fatty," was among the contenders and, since I wanted to meet him, I walked up and introduced myself.

"Hi, I'm Steve Lillis."

"Hi, Steve. I know who you are." (This was back in the days when I was considered a top pool player.)

"Well, Fatty, I just wanted to meet you and say hi. I've seen you from a distance here and there, but I wanted to talk to you personally and shake your hand."

Accustomed to people seeking the privilege of his introduction, he extended his hand in a friendly gesture. As I prepared to courteously move on, Fatty asked me a question.

"How would you like to join me in my trick shot show in about an hour?"

"Really? Are you serious? Yeah! Of course I would!"

"Okay. Come to the table in the main arena in forty-five minutes. We'll do a trick shot show together. You don't need to say or do anything. Just follow my lead."

"Thank you! I'll be there!"

I could not believe it. Minnesota Fats was going to allow me to assist him in one of his famous trick shot shows! I knew this was a once in a life time experience. He was one of the most famous men in the country and attracted pool players and non-pool players alike to his performances. Less than forty-five minutes later, I was waiting at the designated meeting place peering out at hundreds of onlookers who were biding their time until the show started.

Rudolf was the ultimate story teller and everyone was drawn into his escapades as if he was, in reality, Minnesota Fats. Even though the audience knew he was telling yarns, they easily allowed themselves to be reeled in just because of the way he could tell a story. Being on stage alongside of him, I watched in fascination as he seemed to read the audience.

As for my part in the show, I was allowed to shoot a couple of shots, take balls out of their pockets, and be the brunt of a few jokes. As for the show's impact in my life? I learned how to have a conversation with an audience. Watching the people from the stage perspective, I could see how Rudolf took his cues from their facial expressions. He listened to their laughter or silence and responded accordingly in a manner which kept them on the edge of their seats. His presentation employed interactive drama rather than rote scripting.

After the show, Fatty said, "Thank you," but I was the one who was thankful. At the time, I had no clue that I might one day be performing my own trick shot shows, but the memory of this experience positively impacted the development of my style. I learned the art of storytelling and how to draw in a crowd from Minnesota Fats.

Getting the crowd to show up in the first place proved to be difficult after my dad was gone and my mother no longer was a missionary with SOWERS. For over a year they had told me where to be and when to be there. My job had simply been to show up, perform the show, and leave. I was not prepared to promote my show to potential venues.

The success of my ministry had obviously been due to my parents. They had led me and I had followed. The simplicity of my actions mimicked the trust which I knew God was teaching me to use. Typically, when I had not known how to proceed in life, I had turned to God in exasperation and prayed, "What do you want me to do?" However, I could no longer ask that question because I knew what God wanted me to do. He wanted me to play pool for Him. The question now was "How?" For the first time, I prayed, "Lord, how can you use me?"

His answer has directed my ministry to this day. He was going to fulfill the role of my parents by telling me where to be and when to be there. I would just have to watch for the opportunities and then show up. The Lord would lead me and I would follow. Allow me to explain the first of many God ordained appointments which I have experienced.

While pursuing my master's degree, I had also involved myself with the InterVarsity Christian Fellowship campus ministry where I became good friends with Reverend Ken Vander Wall. Ken came to me with a suggestion one day.

155

"Steve, we are going to have students from about twenty five different schools meeting in the area for an InterVarsity Regional meeting. Since the church we are meeting at has a pool table, why don't you do a short Gospel Trick Shot presentation for the college students to see if they're interested?"

"Sure. I've never done anything for college kids before. Let's give it a try."

After my twenty minute show at Ken's meeting, students literally lined up with requests. "We have been looking for a way to reach students on our campus. Please come to our school and do what you just did on our pool table."

God became my new booking agent. With one performance, He had completely filled my calendar for the next year with shows at colleges and universities throughout the region.

Unfortunately, I was no longer getting free room and board from my parents and the travel expenses were quickly causing me to go broke. Before I could complain, God solved the problem by bringing across my path Robert F. Conley, Esquire whose office was located in Fair Lawn, New Jersey. He said, "Steve, you can't keep spending your own money. I'm a lawyer. Let me incorporate you."

"Incorporate me?"

"Of course. People in churches will never give money to a pool player." (He did not have to convince me on that point.) "They will be more comfortable giving tax deductible donations to a pool ministry."

I had never considered receiving donations. As long as I had a job and income, my plan had been to use my own money. However, the increased demand and time commitment within the ministry had been taking its toll.

Intrigued with the idea, I asked, "How much does it cost to incorporate?"

"Steve, I'm going to pay for it and I'm going to do all of the paperwork. You don't have to do anything but say 'Yes.'"

"Okay, let's do it."

On June 8, 1998, my pool playing ministry became Gospel Trick Shot Ministries, Incorporated. Nine men became my board members and I submitted myself to their wise counsel. Reverend

Ken Vander Wall from the InterVarsity ministry was on my original board and remains a faithful board member to this day.

With God's faithful provision of new financial support from my church, campus ministries, and individual friends, I was able to fulfill my calendar show commitments. With more hours available during the weekdays, I advanced both my secular and religious education. I earned an additional undergraduate degree in Computer Science and accepted a position as an English professor at Passaic County Community College. One year later, I was offered a position at William Paterson University as Adjunct Professor of Computer Science which I graciously accepted. By the year 2000, I also received a diploma in Bible accompanied with a teaching certificate.

At present, I am an Adjunct Professor of English and I continue to teach classes at Passaic County Community College, William Paterson University, and Kean University. In addition, I am still performing Gospel Trick Shot shows for colleges, universities, churches, and many other venues typically outside the realm of traditional pool environments.

When Hawthorne Gospel Church commissioned me as a "missionary" in the fall of 2000, my plan was to continue preaching primarily to the non-pool playing population. I was not prepared for God to pave a pathway which led directly into the heart of the billiard industry. He was also going to send me to the pool players as the "Pastor of Pool."

CHAPTER 21

"I love all who love me.
Those who search for me will surely find me."
(Proverbs 8:17)

As far as the pool world was concerned, I was a forgotten has been. Without warning, I had dropped out of the competitive arena when Camille had left me back in 1985. However, news about my ministry apparently began to spread through the pool playing community because I received a phone call one day in 1998 from professional player Robin Bell Dodson (who would be inducted into both the 2005 BCA Hall of Fame and the 2009 WPBA Hall of Fame).[18]

Robin had also become a Christian and we shared a similar testimony of leaving a lifestyle of drugs to embrace God's love and forgiveness. Our conversation centered on how we could use our pool talents to serve the Lord and I pondered what God might be planning.

A few months later, another professional pool player, Tom "Dr. Cue" Rossman, called me. The nickname "Dr. Cue" came from his desire to be an M.D. (doctor of medicine), but instead he chose to become a B.D. (doctor of billiardology). For those unfamiliar with Tom's term, "Billiardology" is the study of spheres, projectiles, and planes; better known as billiard balls, cue sticks, and pool tables.

Tom's phone call created a stir of excitement within me because of his growing resume of Artistic Pool and Trick Shot achievements. He not only held the 1982 World Masters Trick Shot Champion title, but would accumulate many more titles including:

ESPN Trick Shot Magic Champion - 2002/2008
WPA World Artistic Pool Champion - 2006

US Open Artistic Pool Champion - 2007
World Cup Of Trick Shots (Team USA) Champion -
    2006/2008/2009[19]

Why was Tom calling me? I humbly listened as Tom shared his own ministry vision. "Steve, I've heard about your ministry and I think it's great what you are doing. Back in 1984, I also started a ministry called "R.A.C.K." which stands for Recreational Ambassadors for Christ's Kingdom. The purpose is to improve the image of pocket billiards in a manner so that we may all enjoy, share, care, and understand the true meaning of love. Love for God, love of fellow players, love of friends, and love of our sport. I'm looking forward to seeing how God also uses Gospel Trick Shot Ministries to share His love with others within the billiard industry."

Tom's encouragement allowed my thoughts to drift toward the possibility of doing Gospel Trick Shot shows directly within the billiard community. However, since no one in the industry knew me anymore, how could I credibly reappear? Another phone call provided a clue.

"Steve," an edge of excitement accompanied Tom's voice, "I'm helping to develop the first WPA World Artistic Pool Championship at the Las Vegas 2000 BCA Pool League event in May. Would you like to come and compete in a BCA North American 'World Qualifier' prior to and for the World Championship?"

Needless to say, I answered, "Yes!" Because of the expenses associated with participating in professional tournaments, most players receive help from sponsors. Amazingly, members from my church, Hawthorne Gospel, offered to send me. God had faithfully placed me in that *"rare church which would endorse a pool playing missionary."*

Prepared to share the vision of Gospel Trick Shot Ministries with anyone who would listen, I found myself nervously walking through the lobby door of the Riviera Hotel where the tournament was being held. My apprehension was short lived, however, because who did God have *"coincidently"* walking right at me? None other than my old friend Mike Massey!

159

We had not seen or talked to each other since 1985 when he was spiraling downhill in depression and about to lose his family and business. I soon learned he had suffered a breakdown, but two caring friends had taken him in and nursed him back to health. His pool career was now climbing to new heights and he was happily remarried. In addition, he was once again renewing his faith. The old Mike was back and he had even added a new twist to his testimony which he still employs to this day. Whenever he is asked for his autograph, Mike also pens the inscription "Jesus loves us" next to his name.

Mike and I hugged like two long lost buddies. After giving each other a brief update on our lives, Mike grabbed my arm and said, "Steve, come on. I'm going to introduce you to everybody in the building." And to think, I had been worried about how I could credibly reappear! I'm sure God was smiling as I experienced another lesson learned.

For the next three hours, Mike literally walked me to every vendor booth in the arena and said, "Steve Lillis is back and he's a preacher now!" If people had forgotten who I was or never knew who I was, they knew now! Everyone became aware of my position as a preacher and with that came my personal responsibility to live a godly life within an environment which is typically marked by ungodliness as my own testimony revealed.

I was by no means perfect. Sometimes I helped people because of my failures and sometimes I hurt people because of my failures. My faith did not change me to become sinless, but rather gave me the motivation and power to sin less.

Mike Massey won the 2000 BCA World Artistic Pool Qualifier and then won the 2000 WPA World Artistic Pool Championship title in the same venue. I only finished 7th in the BCA World Qualifier event, but I received a prize more valuable than a trophy. God had used me to lead Bible studies which in turn began to bring together many of the Christian pool players scattered throughout the industry. I was not able to perform a show that year, but I have performed a Gospel Trick Shot show at the BCA Pool League tournament every year since.

Before the next tournament in 2001 arrived, I received another phone call from Tom. "Steve, I can't be a contestant and run the event at the same time because it would be a conflict of interest. I need somebody to run artistic pool who will not also compete. Would you consider taking the position even though it means that you would not be able to play?"

Because preaching, not playing, was now my priority, I answered, "Of course!" I served as Chairman of the WPA "General Artistic Pool Committee" from 2001-2002 and I served as Chairman of the WPA Artistic Pool Division from 2002-2004. Many members from my church rallied together as sponsors and contributed tens of thousands of dollars toward sending helpers along with me who kept score, set up the arena, taped video, and assisted with many other tasks necessary to run a successful tournament. These same men and women also managed our Gospel Trick Shot Ministries booth where hundreds of Bibles were given away along with towels, hats, door prizes, Cue4Christ products, and CPPA shirts (CPPA is the *Christian Pool Players Association* founded by Jim Mazzulla). The willingness of the church constituency to endorse pool as well as the willingness of pool players to receive the church's involvement was unprecedented. The dichotomy of the two institutions converged as a team working together to promote the integrity of the sport.

A group of us also produced an elaborate Gospel Trick Shot Ministries performance which was offered free of charge to anyone who wanted to come. The two hour show, complete with printed programs, included Gospel singing, entertaining trick shots, and life testimonies. Mike Massey, LoreeJon (Jones) Hasson (2002 BCA Hall of Fame inductee), and Steve Geller (1979-1980 BCA Trick Shot champion) led the Gospel singing. Tom Rossman, Mike Massey, and I performed trick shots and Robin Dodson, Mike Massey, and I shared testimonies. The Master of Ceremonies was Jeff Ballantyne, the pool player who had chosen to "quit pool and go to Bible school" after I had unwittingly shared the Gospel with him years ago in Colorado Springs. God was faithfully tying the loose ends of my life together. In the years following, others joined the stage including:

Belinda Campos Calhoun - 2006 WPBA Hall of Fame.

Jim Rempe - 2002 BCA Hall of Fame inductee and well known for his training cue ball.

Bob Meucci - founder of Meucci Cues.

Tommy Kennedy – holder of more than 130 tournament titles and known as the most affable player on the professional tour because he is always ready with a smile and hug for everyone.

The endorsement of Gospel Trick Shot Ministries, Inc. from these great players opened the doors for many more shows to be performed nationwide at other billiard venues and tournaments. Hundreds of people have come to Christ or rededicated their lives. God has done amazing things and Gospel Trick Shot artists are continuing to multiply with young players such as Jason "The Michigan Kid" Lynch, Robby "The Hurricane" Peacock, Rodney "Triple P" (Pool Playing Pastor) Fontaine, Wayne Parker of South Africa, Brian "Superman" Pauley, and Pastor Michael "Man of the Simonis Cloth" Hewitt of New Life Community Church in Wayland, Michigan.

It has not been easy delivering the Gospel message to the pool world. Hecklers abound. A five year old child reminded me recently of my Chattanooga shoemaker friend and his words of wisdom from Ephesians 6:12, "For we wrestle not against flesh and blood, but against powers and principalities, against spiritual wickedness in high places, against rulers of the unseen dark domain."

This became clear in a session at the University of Texas El Paso where I went to perform a Gospel Trick Shot show. The campus ministry leaders had also scheduled me to perform at one of their local pool rooms. Not being familiar with the establishment, the leaders brought their two children. One was a five year old little girl.

As a traveling missionary, I never know what to expect, but over the years I have learned how to read the room with one glance at my audience. When I walked into this pool room, I knew trouble was in my future. Loud music, loosely clad women, and drunken men painted the scene. The portrait did not get much better when

162

the waitress explained the manager's temporary absence and she knew nothing about a Gospel Trick Shot show. However, she was accommodating and gave us a table next to some girls attempting to play in a manner meant to attract the attention of the men at the bar.

I felt bad for my ministry hosts as they looked at their watches to see if any of the invited guests would show up. No one did. The time came when I was supposed to start the show and my only "friendly" audience was the two ministry leaders, their two children, and one of the student leaders from the campus. Most people would give up and say, "Let's go." Even though my hosts considered the option, God had taught me how to follow His lead. I was at His "when and where" and I submitted. Knowing I was about to sacrifice myself to the wolves and the innocent ministry leaders were about to witness a feeding frenzy, I faithfully pursued whatever purpose God wanted to use me for and I prepared my props.

True to my expectations, the heckling began as I started my show. The girls playing next to me began to giggle louder as they intentionally bent over the pool table more than necessary to accomplish their intended shots. The group of guys at the bar swiveled around to watch, but were not quiet about their opinions of God. One of the guys in particular was being exceptionally boisterous. In fact, my typical ability to patiently endure these situations was reaching its limit and boiled over when he shouted, *"I have no interest in going to heaven. I WANT to go to hell."*

A silent gasp captured the lungs of everyone within listening distance. The possible truth of what I had been preaching suddenly stung everyone in the heart. No one wanted to go to hell. Hearing someone shout his preference to go to hell was sobering. I watched as even his buddies sitting at the bar protectively drew their drinks closer in an attempt to distance themselves from such a foreign desire.

God had set the stage. His audience was listening, but my anger was still boiling. The wrestling feud between the powers of good and evil had begun and the ensuing match was legit. Attempting to take down my opponent, I heatedly called, *"And unless you choose to believe in God as your Savior and repent from your sins, hell is exactly where you are going to go when you die!"*

If I thought the first gasp had filled everyone's lungs, everyone was surprised to learn that even more air could fit in! Even the waitress was responding by turning the loud music down. With the room silently tense, I proceeded with my demonstration. One trick shot told about God's love while another told about God's offer of forgiveness for those who believe. By the time I performed the last shot depicting God's desire to give us eternal life in heaven so that we do not have to go to hell, everyone in the pool room had gathered around to listen.

As I ended the show, the waitress came up and whispered something in my ear. I smiled and then announced, "After I close in prayer, free pizza is available at the bar for anyone who would like some." The manager apparently was offering his amends for not being available when we arrived.

While everyone made a mad dash for the pizza as soon as they heard the word "Amen," the hell bound young man jumped off of his barstool and came at me.

"Why did you do that?"

"Do what?" I assumed he was talking about my angry threat to his bold declaration and I was cautiously trying to avoid a re-match.

"Why did you give us free pizza? After all of our rudeness and attempts to mess up your show, you offer us free pizza? Why?!"

Pizza! I inwardly chuckled at the strange ways of my God. Who would have thought that a slice of free pizza would open this young man's heart? Acting as God's delivery man, I said, "The free pizza is like God's free gift of eternal life. We expect to pay for pizza just as our inner soul expects to one day pay for our bad deeds. But just like your pizza was paid for, Jesus already paid the death penalty for your sin when He died in your place on the cross. Jesus said, 'I am the resurrection and the life. Those who believe in me, even though they die like everyone else, will live again. They are given eternal life for believing in me.' God is freely offering you His love and forgiveness. If you believe, then He will give you eternity in heaven and you will escape hell. The decision is yours. Do you believe?"

164

The young man listened and then, with tears in his eyes, he said, "Yes. I not only believe, but I want to do what you do. I want to tell people that God loves them."

As I was packing up my props getting ready to leave, the ministry leader's little five year old girl came up to me at the pool table and tugged at my pant leg. I squatted down and soon had tears welling up in my own eyes as she uttered two simple words. "God won."

Out of the mouth of babes. She was right. I served a powerful God. Who would have ever thought that the most aggressive verbal opponent in the audience would be the one to repent? God did and He had won the young man's heart.

Through the years, I have continued to perform hundreds of Gospel Trick Shot shows both inside and outside of the billiard industry. I also returned to playing competitive 9-Ball where I ranked in the top 32 players from 2003-2008 according to the UPA rankings with sanctioning by the BCA. In 2004, I was even chosen as one of thirteen to represent the United States in Taiwan at the WPA World 9-Ball Championships.

God had moved me into the mainstream of competitive pool which allowed me to mix with professionals around the world. Many top pool players have heard the Gospel message in one venue or another because God allowed me, the prodigal pool player, to share His message with others. In 2007, I was appointed as the Chaplain of the UPA Professional Men's Pro Tour. God was officially using my love for the sport of billiards to serve Him.

CHAPTER 22

"Hope deferred makes the heart sick,
but when dreams come true, there is life and joy."
(Proverbs 13:12)

"Dad, you can't forget 7-11! It's like the store!" Amanda was giddy with excitement. My oldest daughter was getting married on July 11, 2008. About the same time, my youngest daughter, Sarah, announced the news that I was going to be a grandpa. Time had stolen the youth of my children.

Despite my attempts to rewind the clock, "7-11" arrived quickly. Sarah was nine months along when she marched down the aisle as Amanda's bridesmaid and her beautiful baby boy was born only nine days later on July twentieth. His name was Jayden and God would use my first grandson as the catalyst to heal my broken relationship with family. Not surprisingly, the American meaning of the name *Jayden* is "God has heard."[20] God had been listening.

The festivities bustled around me as I sat at a lone reception table after the wedding. I watched my family and wondered, "What does the future hold for all of us?"

Amanda had found her love in life. His name was Tim and he would soon become the youth minister at their church. I felt at peace regarding her marriage and I praised God for leading her to a godly man.

Sarah was anticipating the joys of motherhood. Although she would soon marry Jayden's father, I worried about her life and prayed for God to protect her.

Camille continued to show signs of drug addiction. She was still under a doctor's care for her struggles with post partum depression and the mental breakdown she had experienced. In addition, she suffered with Fibromyalgia. The combination of the various treatment drugs prescribed had sadly led to her addiction to pain medications. Camille was in need of help, but she would have to make the decision to submit herself to it.

I learned a few weeks later of Camille's effort to change. Similar to the couple who took in Mike Massey and nursed him through his depression, some caring friends, who have requested to remain anonymous, invited Camille to their home located in another state for the purpose of holding her accountable through an attempt at detoxification. Surprisingly, Camille agreed and placed herself in their care by packing up and moving into their secluded home.

My own life was also experiencing a change. Even though I had always taken every opportunity to spend time with family whenever I was allowed, for the first time since the girls were babies, I felt the warmth of fatherhood. Tim and Amanda welcomed me into their home with frequent dinner invitations and Sarah's desire to share Jayden's growth allowed me many opportunities to see her and my grandson.

Experiencing my own joy in Jayden, I knew Camille must be missing her new grandson as well as feeling severed from her daughters. She had never been apart from Amanda and Sarah before. When Christmas 2008 arrived, I gave my car keys to the girls and suggested they pay their mother a surprise visit. They immediately conspired in a plan, and I contentedly waved goodbye as I watched Amanda, Tim, Sarah, and Jayden drive off for the holidays. I knew Camille was about to receive a Christmas blessing.

Within a few days, I received my own blessing. The phone rang and when I answered, Camille was on the other end.

"Hi, Steve. I want to come home. I want to be your wife."

For the past nineteen years, I had dreamed of hearing those words, but upon hearing them said, how was I going to respond? Of course I wanted Camille to come home and be my wife, but it was not that easy! I did not know how her friends felt. Their involvement had been successfully helping Camille work through the pain of drug withdrawal and I did not know whether her addiction had been contained yet. Where would we live? I had been living with another missionary roommate, Hayward Clark, for the past fifteen years in a small two bedroom, one bath apartment in Paterson, New Jersey. My calendar was filled with upcoming Gospel Trick Shot shows and I had to be back at work in a few days when the spring semester started. I was not ready for my wife to come home and I tried my best to explain.

"Camille, honey, I want you to come home, but now is not the right time."

"I want to come home now, Steve. I can ride back with the girls. I miss them. I miss Jayden."

"I understand, but you can't just pack up and leave. You have made a commitment to your friends who are helping you to get better. If you come back before you are ready, it would be another uphill battle between us."

"You're probably right, but what can I do? I'm not happy here."

"I'll start working on a plan to drive down and pick you up. In the meantime, just keep taking care of yourself."

I hung up the phone in disbelief. God had heard my prayers. Memories of a radio broadcast brought an additional smile to my soul. During the early days of my ministry, in 2001, I had declared my hope of Camille's return on the "Words to Live By" show produced by Radio Bible Class of Grand Rapids, Michigan (RBC Ministries). The host had invited me to share my story as a modern day Biblical example of Hosea.

Hosea was a man faithful to his wife despite her unfaithfulness. His story comparatively symbolized the unfaithfulness of God's people versus God's faithfulness to wait expectantly for His people to return to Him. I not only related to Hosea's life as a husband with my hope of Camille's return, I also related to the unfaithfulness which Hosea's wife represented. Throughout my life, I had been unfaithful to God in my sinful actions and yet God was always faithfully waiting to receive me again every time I returned with my repentant heart. God's love was, and is, never-ending.

Even though Camille was not yet by my side, I was at peace. Days turned into weeks as I developed a plan which would bring my wife home by the summer. By then, my school semester would be over and my Gospel Trick Shot calendar cleared because

I was not scheduling any new events. I wanted to spend un-distracted time with my wife upon her return.

Other than a national pool tournament in May, one of the last items on my calendar was the Mayor's prayer breakfast on Good Friday, April 10, 2009. I had been invited as the featured speaker for the purpose of sharing about my pool ministry travels around the world. I thought my speech was prepared until events happened three days earlier on Tuesday, April 7, 2009. Amanda called me.

"Dad! Mom's coming!"

"What do you mean 'Mom's coming?'"

"She's coming home."

"How? She has no car and she has no money. It's not time yet! She knows I'm going to bring her home when the semester is over at the end of May."

"I don't know, Dad, but she's coming!"

I hung up the phone with confusion swirling through my mind. Was Camille really on her way? The phone rang again and I jumped to answer.

"Mom's at a hotel in Virginia. She took her friends' car and credit card! They're angry and even threatening to have her arrested. Oh Dad! What are we going to do?"

"Amanda," I tried to remain calm, but the fear of Camille's incarceration was not something I was ready to deal with, "please, get your mother to call me. Maybe I can get her to turn around."

"She only wants to talk to me, Dad. She doesn't want to talk with anyone else."

"Please Amanda, she listens to you. Get her to call me!"

We hung up again and I trembled by the phone. I was praying, but only God could have made sense of my jumbled thoughts. Once again the phone rang.

"Hi, Steve, it's me."

"Camille! I don't know what's going on, but you have to take the car back. Your friends are hopping mad and they are possibly going to have you arrested. You've got to turn the car around and head back."

"But I don't want to go back! You don't know what they're doing to me! Don't make me go back there. Please!"

"This is not the way to do it, Camille. You've got to turn around."

Silence spoke to me on the phone for the next minute until Camille said with a tone of resignation, "Okay, I'll head back tomorrow."

"Thank you, Camille. I know you don't want to go back, but it's the best thing to do. Call me as soon as you get there."

The next day, Wednesday, I waited anxiously for the phone to ring and when I answered it, Amanda was speaking in a tentative tone. Her words were not what I was expecting.

"Dad, Mom is here in New Jersey and she's checked into a local hotel. She drove back, but instead of going back to her friends' house, she left their car at the local airport and used their credit card to buy a plane ticket. What should I do?"

"Bring her here to my apartment."

Camille crossed my threshold with Amanda at her side at around 6:00 in the evening. Sarah also came and the four of us sat in the living room together, alone, for the first time in years. We were quietly tense, not knowing what to say until a phone call spurred our conversation.

"Hello?" My ear drums, which had been the only part of me to relax in the silent room, were now drumming loudly as her friend's angry voice resonated through the phone lines.

"Steve! I know she's there. Before she digs herself into an even deeper hole, I want that credit card back! I also want the $1500 she spent returned and I want it paid back NOW! Otherwise, I'm coming up there and I'm going to have her arrested. You know I can and I will. Don't make me do it."

The threat was loud and clear. Everyone in the room could hear the conversation. As the voice continued to rant and rave on the phone, I witnessed a healing wash over Camille as she began to sob.

"I'm sorry. I didn't mean to make everyone mad, but I felt like a prisoner. They wouldn't let me have my own money and they wouldn't let me go anywhere. I had to escape. I had to get away. I need you. Please let me stay."

Camille sat before us as a broken woman beseeching our love and we all willingly gave it to her. At that very moment, the four of us experienced the unity of a family which has remained unbroken to this day.

With the angry voice of Camille's friend still audible through the phone, our family supportively came together.

"I'll pay $500." One of my daughters offered.

"I'll pay $500." My other daughter immediately added.

"And I'll pay $500," I announced as I put the phone back up to my ear and said, "We'll send you the money along with the return of your credit card. Your car is at the airport with the keys in it."

The hour was getting late and, even though I knew Camille had checked into a hotel because she did not know how I would react to her premature arrival, I did not want her staying somewhere else. Her home was with me. We all went to the hotel room and brought her suitcases back to the apartment. With all of our emotions exhausted, the girls went home and Camille and I were left alone. Awkwardly, because I did not know what else to do, I said, "I'm sure you're tired, too. Until we can work out something, I'll fix up the couch for you to sleep on."

As I lay wide awake in my room, I pondered God's miraculous gift. My wife had come home!

The next morning, Thursday, I received a phone call from one of my ministry supporters who was aware of my plans to reunite with Camille after the school semester ended in May. Having no clue that Camille had already returned the night before, he said, "Steve, I know your plans to bring Camille home and I don't want your finances to be a hindrance in your adjustment. I'm going to give the ministry $30,000 to help you with the transition."

I melted in humbleness to the Lord. He had not only heard, but He had provided. Upon sharing with Camille what this precious man had given to us, she wept. We both felt God's healing touch through the timing of this man's phone call. God's desire for our marriage to survive was clear.

When bedtime came on Thursday night, I once again lay wide awake in my room pondering God's miraculous gift. My wife had not only come home, but God had provided the means for me to care for her. As I was praising God for all of the good things He was doing in my life, I heard a knock on my door.

171

"Steve," Camille timidly whispered, "I can't sleep on the couch. Can I please come in with you? I promise I won't do anything."

Before I could answer, she came in and slipped under the covers at the far edge of the bed. As she lay facing the wall, Camille began to softly cry, "I'm sorry, Steve. I'm sorry."

I gently drew Camille toward me and we embraced.

"It's okay, sweetheart. It's okay. I love you."

The next morning, April 10, 2009, was the Mayor's Good Friday prayer breakfast. Needless to say, my prepared speech was thrown out of the proverbial window. Everything I had planned to say about my world travels, about my ministry accomplishments, and about my pool playing career paled in comparison to the miracle of my wife's return and the restoration of my family. As I stood behind the podium, I saw Camille, Amanda, Tim, Sarah, Jayden's father, and Jayden seated at our table. It was the first time we were all together united as a family and it was the first time I joyfully shared my life story with others.

Two days later, on Resurrection Sunday, our family sat together during the Easter church service and each one of us knew that God had resurrected the life of our family. A new life journey stretched ahead and my heart was "leapin" with joy!

Epilogue

"Mom, you look beautiful!" The girls chimed in unison. "Dad is going to be grinning ear to ear when he sees you walking down the aisle."

On Sunday, April 25, 2010, in a small little country church where my daughter sang in the choir and my son-in-law was the youth leader, Camille and I stood at the altar in a "Renewal of Vows" ceremony celebrating 30 years of marriage. We were not concerned with our 19 years, 5 months, 16 days, and 3 hours of separation, but rather joyously celebrated with our family and friends God's faithfulness to bring us back together.

Not only has our marriage continued to be surrounded by God's tender mercies, but Camille has joined me in many of my Gospel Trick Shot Ministries adventures. We have become a team working together to share God's unfailing love with others. Not too long ago, Camille said something to me which I will never forget: "If God had not allowed us to be separated for the past nineteen years, then we would not have this ministry together today."

Praise the Lord for my wife, Camille, and our daughters, Amanda and Sarah, who God continues to use to help shape me and mold me into a kind of man that my Lord and Savior Jesus Christ can use for His glory and honor!

"Trust in the Lord with all your heart;
do not depend on your own understanding.
Seek His will in all you do,
and He will direct your paths."
(Proverbs 3:5-6)

Thoughts From The Co-Author

My enjoyment of writing can be attested to by the many friends and business associates who have received my long winded emails and written correspondence. However, writing a book was only a dream appearing on my "bucket list." I never thought that I could or would achieve this goal, but I guess I am now officially ready to "kick."

I met Steve in May, 2009, one month after God miraculously reunited his family. As time progressed, Steve shared his desire to write his story and I offered to help. Steve flew out to California and on the day he would begin narrating his story, I wrote *"3-15-11, Steve starts dictating book"* next to the following verse in my morning Bible reading:

> "For the Kingdom of God is not just fancy talk;
> it is living by God's power."
> (1 Corinthians 4:20)

For those who know Steve personally, he is a showman fully capable of drawing in his listeners with fancy talk. As I listened to his story, though, I heard the escapades of a wayward man searching for purpose and meaning in life. My task was not going to be for the purpose of entertaining the reader, but rather to demonstrate how we can live by God's power despite our human failures.

After Steve flew home, I began the task of transcribing his story. I had not realized my memory skills were significantly failing. I would listen to a sentence, turn off the tape recorder, and then find I could barely remember three words! I struggled through the transcription process. Sensing my feelings of futility, God gave me another Scripture. I wrote, *"3-23-11, transcribing almost done"* next to the following verse in my morning Bible reading:

> "So, my dear brothers and sisters, be strong and steady,
> always enthusiastic about the Lord's work, for you know
> that nothing you do for the Lord is ever useless."
> (1 Corinthians 15:58)

The verse served to encourage me despite my feelings of being overwhelmed. With over fifty single spaced pages of transcribed narration, how was I going to start? I was not a professional author. God would have to guide my hands. My logic was simple: *If God could guide the hands of the Bible writers to tell His story, then God could guide my hands to tell Steve's story.*

Shortly after completing the transcription process, I sat down one Sunday morning before church to begin writing. I bowed my head and I simply prayed, "God, this is your book. Please guide my hands to tell your story."

Amazingly, the "hustling episode" on the first three pages of the book flowed through my fingers onto the computer screen. I excitedly drove to church that morning praising God for His help.

Months passed and I continued to make progress. However, when March 2012 approached, I was nearing the end of the book. I began to think, "*If people ask me how long it took to write the book, I want to be able to say that it took one year.*" This thought motivated me to finish quickly. I began spending about five to six hours a day and when March 31st arrived, I emailed the last chapter to Steve for his approval.

I only wished that I had remembered the actual date of the morning on which I had written those first three pages. In His kindness, God chose to grant my wish. On April 4, 2012, I found the following note in my daily Bible reading which I had written almost a year earlier in my Bible's margin:

> "*Remember my enthusiasm to write the first three pages of Steve's book and use it to help me finish - even though I know I will hit writer's block!*
> *First pages written 4-10-11.*"

When I saw the date, "*4-10-11,*" I was excited. I had written proof that I had finished the book within my one year goal! I eagerly read the verse which was underlined next to the encouraging message I had written to myself.

"I suggest that you finish what you started a year ago,
for you were the first to propose this idea,
and you were the first to begin doing something about it.
Now you should carry this project through to completion
just as enthusiastically as you began it."
(2 Corinthians 8:10-11)

Wow!!! A year ago, I had used this verse to motivate me to remain faithful to finish Steve's book and one year later, the project was complete. I excitedly emailed Steve, telling him about my handwritten note and I patted myself proudly on the back for completing the task within my goal of one year.

Even though I had just written the powerful last chapter of Steve's book, I had already forgotten. Most likely, if you are reading this, you have forgotten also. Steve emailed me back and simply said,

Yes, April 10th is a very special day. It was April 10, 2009, when my family was united together at the Mayor's Good Friday prayer breakfast.

Our God is an awesome God. He coordinated my start date of the book exactly on the date on which He knew the story would culminate. God had indeed guided my fingers.

And the day I am writing these thoughts?
Good Friday, April 6, 2012.

"It is Finished." (John 19:30)

Praise the Lord!
Devra Robledo

Bachelor of Science in Business Administration at Biola University
Accounting and Biblical Studies Concentration
Master of Business Administration at California State University, Fullerton
Marketing Concentration
President, Wildlife in Wood, Inc. and SOURCEnterprises, Inc.
Co-Inventor of Bobble Ball, the egg shaped billiard ball
Co-Inventor of the DiRiginal Portable Pool Table

Steve Lillis
<u>Personal Credits and Titles:</u>

1977 - represented the U.S. Navy in world championship competitions and finished in the top ten in the World 14.1 Straight Pool and the World 9 Ball Championships

1979 - BCA Colorado State 8 Ball Champion

1980 - BCA Georgia State 9 Ball Champion

1981 - Miller Lite Tennessee State 8 Ball Champion

1981 - Miller Lite Tennessee State 9 Ball Champion

1981 - Miller Lite Southeastern 8 Ball Champion

1981 - Miller Lite Southeastern 9 Ball Champion

1982 - BCA Florida State 9 Ball Champion

1985-1996 - in retirement from playing professional pool

2000 – came out of retirement to compete in the first ever BCA North American Artistic Pool Championship, which was a "world qualifier" for the first ever WPA World Artistic Pool Championship.

2001 - 2002 – served as Chairman of the World Pool Billiard Association (WPA) "General Artistic Pool Committee."

2002-2004 – served as Chairman of the World Pool Billiard Association Artistic Pool Division (WPA APD)

2003 - 2008 - ranked in the top 32 according to the UPA (United States Professional Pool Players Association) rankings with sanctioning by the BCA (Billiard Congress of America)

2004 - Picked by the BCA to represent the United States in Taipei City, Taiwan at the WPA (World Pool and Billiard Association) World 9 Ball Championships

2006 - invited by Albanian Billiard Federation to teach 12 pro Albanian pool players and coaches and design and perform a TV pool show for *Telesports,* their major sports network

2007 - selected to be the UPA Chaplain of the men's professional tour and confirmed by the BCA

6/2008 - Steve Lillis ranked in the top 32 players was invited to play in the BCA GenerationPool.com 9 Ball ESPN TV tournament in Charlotte, NC and performed a Gospel Trick Shot Show for the live TV audience

Gospel Trick Shot Ministries, Inc.
Colleges And Universities Visited

Campus Ministries:

InterVarsity Christian Fellowship
Campus Ambassadors
International Student Friendship Ministries
Campus Crusade for Christ
Chi Alpha Christian Fellowship

New Jersey Schools:

William Paterson University
Farleigh Dickenson University
Essex County Community College
Montclair State University
New Jersey Institute of Technology
Passaic County Community College
Drew University
Ramapo College of New Jersey
Rutgers University in New Brunswick
Rutgers Newark
Princeton University
Kean University
New Jersey City University
Caldwell College

Other Colleges and Universities:

Southern Illinois University
Bradley University in IL

University of Minnesota
North Central University in MN
Saint Mary's University in MN
Winona State University in MN

University of Texas El Paso
Texas A & M University
Lamar University in TX

Arizona State University

State University of New York SUNY Plattsburgh
State University of New York SUNY Cortland
Nassau County Community College in NY
Ithaca College in NY
Nyack College in NY
Fashion Institute of Technology in NY
Rensellear Polytechnic Institute in NY

University of South Florida
University of Maryland
University of New Hampshire
Massachusetts Institute of Technology
Valley Forge Christian College in PA

Gospel Trick Shot Ministries, Inc.
Countries Visited Outside
<u>North America:</u>

England 2001

Germany 2002, 2004

Albania 2003, 2006, 2007

Ukraine 2003

Taiwan 2004

Korea 2004

China 2005, 2012

Greece 2007

Russia 2007

Dubai & Abu Dhabi of the United Arab Emirates UAE 2009

Kuwait 2009

Bahrain 2009

Tanzania 2010

Kenya 2010, 2012

Egypt 2010, 2011

Iraq 2012

Philippines 2012

Honduras 2012

Gospel Trick Shot Ministries, Inc.
Credits and Accomplishments:

6/1998 - Gospel Trick Shot Ministries, Inc. was incorporated.

8/1998 - Steve Lillis did a GTS (Gospel Trick Shot) show as a part of the 1998 Hawthorne Gospel Church Summer Bible Conference in which such people as Billy Graham of BGEA, Jack Wyrtzen of Word of Life Ministries, Ron Hutchcraft of RHM Ministries, and other worldwide Christian Statesmen have appeared in years past. This was the first major public GTS show.

5/2000, 5/2001, 5/2002, 5/2003, 5/2004, 5/2005, 5/2006, 5/2007, 5/2008, 5/2009, 5/2010, 5/2011, 5/2012 - GTS RACK Team (Recreational Ambassadors for Christ's Kingdom) appeared at the BCA National Eight Ball Championship and Expo in the Riviera Hotel in Las Vegas, Nevada for shows and outreach. Mike Massey, Tom "Dr. Cue" Rossman, and Steve Lillis were the featured performers for most of BCAPL events (Billiard Congress of America Pool League).

2000-2002 - Steve Lillis did GTS Shows at various Joss Northeast Pro Tour events in such states as Connecticut, Maine, New York, and Massachusetts.

2001-2004 - GTS RACK Team appeared at various WPA (World Pool and Billiard Association) World Artistic Pool Tour events for shows and outreach in both the USA and overseas.

3/2002, 3/2003, 3/2004, 3/2005, 3/2006, 3/2007, 3/2008, 3/2009, 3/2010, 3/2011, 3/2012 - GTS RACK Team appeared at the Hopkin's Super Billiard Expo in the Valley Forge Convention Center in Valley Forge, PA for shows and outreach.

8/2002, 8/2003, 8/2004, 8/2005, 8/2006, 8/2007 - GTS RACK Team appeared at the APA (American Poolplayers Association) National Championships in the Riviera Hotel in Las Vegas, NV for shows and outreach.

10/2002, 10/2003, 9/2004, 9/2005 - Steve Lillis did GTS Shows at the NJ State 14.1 Straight Pool Championship in Parsippany, NJ.

12/2002 - Steve Lillis did GTS Shows for the Southeast Pro 9 Ball Tour in Florida.

7/2003, 4/2004, 4/2005, 4/2006, 8/2006, 6/2007, 6/2008, 6/2009, 7/2010 - GTS RACK Team appeared at the BCA (Billiard Congress of America) Trade Shows at various venues for shows and outreach.

2003-2009 - Steve Lillis did GTS Shows at various UPA (United States Professional Poolplayers Association) Tour events in such cities as Phoenix, Philadelphia, Los Angeles, Atlanta, Jacksonville, New York, and Chesapeake, VA at the U.S. Open 9 Ball. Steve has been consistently ranked in the top 32 players in the world on the UPA Tour which was the top professional men's tour from 2003-2008.

10/2003 - GTS RACK Team appeared at the Midwest Billiard Expo in The Pheasant Run Resort in Chicago, IL for shows and outreach.

6/2004 - GTS RACK Team appeared at the VNEA (Valley National Eight Ball Championships in the Riviera Hotel in Las Vegas.

9/2004, 9/2005, 9/2006, 10/2007, 10/2008, 10/2009, 10/2010, 10/2012 - Steve Lillis did a series of GTS Shows at the U.S. Open 9 Ball Championships in the Chesapeake Convention Center in Chesapeake, VA. In 2006 and 2007 Steve was given permission by tournament promoter Barry Berhman to eulogize fallen pool players, share, and pray over the PA system.

10/2004 - Performed Gospel Trick Shot Show at Grand Central Station in New York City.

6/2005 - Steve Lillis performed 14 trick shot shows at the 16th Annual International Sports Show in Shanghai, China.

1/2006 - Steve Lillis was invited by the President of the Albanian Billiard Federation to start a billiard academy with a focus on artistic pool. Steve's title was the "Professor of Bilardo Artistica." The academy was attended by an elite group of players and their coaches called Team Albania.

1/2006 - Steve Lillis performed a Gospel Trick Shot Show on the campus of the University of Tirana in Albania and partnered with Campus Crusade for Christ.

10/2006, 5/2008 - Steve Lillis did a featured GTS presentation at the Hawthorne Gospel Church in Hawthorne, NJ in the "new" gym as part of their 2006 Fall Missions Conference and 2008 Spring Outreach.

2007 - Steve Lillis toured Albania for 3rd time and established and trained a Gospel Trick Shot Team.

1/2007 - Steve Lillis did a series of GTS Shows at the "Derby City Classic" in Louisville, KY working in conjunction with GTS RACK team member Robin Dodson in her booth called Robin's Pro Shop.

11/2007 - Steve Lillis did a series of GTS Shows at the Qlympics Billiard Event in Louisville, KY produced and directed by the BCA Pool League.

1/2008 - Steve Lillis did a series of GTS Shows working in conjunction with Dr. Cue Promotions and the "Classic

Cup" event and the Derby City Classic produced and directed by Diamond Billiard Products. Steve also helped organize and direct the first RACK Room Sunday morning service for pool players and by pool players. GTS/RACK team members Mike Massey, Tom Rossman, and Steve Geller participated.

2009 - Steve Lillis toured the Arabian Peninsula and did a special Gospel Trick Shot Show for the United States Navy 5th fleet on the Island of Bahrain.

12/2009 - Steve Lillis did GTS Shows as part of "Urbana 2009" in St Louis, MO produced and directed by InterVarsity Christian Fellowship which was attended by 17,000 college students.

2009-2012 - GTS RACK Team did GTS Shows at the Christian Sports and Recreation Ministry Summit in Phoenix (2009), Atlanta (2010), Indianapolis (2011), and Dallas (2012).

2010 - Steve Lillis toured East Africa and was selected by the Kenya Pool Club as ambassador for the "Sport for Good" campaign and established and trained a Gospel Trick Shot Team headquartered in Nairobi, Kenya with Jason "The Michigan Kid" Lynch.

12/2010 - Steve did GTS Shows as part of "Radiate 2010" in Baltimore, MD produced and directed by Campus Crusade for Christ which had 1,500 students in attendance.

8/2011 - The GTS RACK Team of Mike Massey, Tom "Dr. Cue" Rossman and Steve Lillis reunite and launch the "RACK Up A Victory" world tour with the first stop at the Hard Rock Hotel in Disney World in Orlando, Florida with a special show to honor the disabled American military veterans returning from Iraq and Afghanistan.

Gospel Trick Shot Ministries, Inc.
<u>Media Credits:</u>

9/2000 and 9/2001 - Steve Lillis was featured on 270 worldwide radio stations as part of RBC's Ministries broadcast entitled "Words to Live By."

2000-2010 - GTS RACK Team members have appeared numerous times on the ESPN broadcast entitled Trick Shot Magic for competition and interviews.

2001-2012 - GTS RACK Team appeared in many newspapers, magazines, brochures, flyers, and other printed material both inside and outside the billiard industry. Steve Lillis appeared on the front page of the June 2004 issue of Professor Q Balls Nationwide Billiard Newspaper.

2/2002 - GTS RACK Team did a show that was taped in Willingen, Germany and broadcast on German Television at the conclusion of the 2002 WPA World Artistic Pool Championship.

3/2002 - GTS RACK Team featured in "Inside Pool" magazine article entitled "GTS RACK Power Team Hits the Road."

6/2003 - GTS RACK Team did a show that was taped in Kiev, Ukraine and broadcast on Russian Television and aired to potentially 290 million people in the former Soviet Union.

12/2003 - Steve Lillis did a GTS Show and interview that was taped by *Telesports* in Tirana, Albania and aired throughout the country of Albania.

8/2004 - Steve Lillis appeared on ESPN TV as the Master of Ceremonies and Head Referee for the 2004 Men's International Challenge of Champions at Mohegan Sun.

8/2004 - Steve Lillis appeared on ESPN TV as the Master of Ceremonies and Head Table Judge for the 2004 Women's International Trick Shot Challenge at Mohegan Sun.

6/2005 - Steve Lillis was interviewed with trick shot show taped for broadcast on Chinese National Television.

1/2006 - Steve Lillis choreographed an artistic billiard show for *Telesports* TV using his own Gospel Trick Shots and included 10 Albanians demonstrating shots they learned at the academy. RACK Team members Tony "The Comic" Anthony, Marcel Kaiser of Germany and Christian Coffey of Canada participated. The three hour broadcast received about 40 hours of air time in Albania.

12/2006 - Steve Lillis was interviewed by David Virkler of Dedication Evangelism for the national radio broadcast of "Word and the World."

12/2006 - Steve Lillis appeared on the national TV broadcast of the "700 Club" on ABC Family and other affiliate television stations. The show was rebroadcast in 2007.

5/2009 - Steve Lillis was featured in billiard publications highlighting a GTS tour of the Arabian Peninsula which included working with mission organizations, U.S. Navy, and the National Billiard Teams of Kuwait, U.A.E., and Bahrain.

6/2010 - Steve Lillis and Jason "The Michigan Kid" Lynch were featured in billiard publications as part of GTS Africa Tour in conjunction with Thomas Aaron Billiards and McDermott Cues. A GTS team of three Kenyans was founded and ongoing Gospel Trick Shot Ministry is in progress in East Africa.

3/2011 – 3/2012 – The life story of Steve Lillis written for future publication.

6/2012 – GTS RACK Team World Tour continues in the Philippines as Mike Massey, Tom "Dr. Cue" Rossman, Scott Pruiskma, and Steve Lillis perform 24 shows in 15 cities on three islands with local, national, and world TV and newspaper coverage. Special interview was done by the 700 Club in their TV studios in Manila.

Bibliography

1. The Holy Bible. Exodus 20:8-10

2. "The Billy Graham New York Crusade, 1957," <u>American Decades</u> 2001. Available at: http://www.encyclopedia.com/doc/1G2-3468302051.html.   13 April 2011

3. "San Francisco to Paris in just two minutes," <u>Daily Mail Reporter</u> (12 April 2011). Available at: http://www.dailymail.co.uk/news/article-1375977/San-Francisco-Paris-just-minutes-Amazing-time-lapse-video-condenses-5-576-miles-into-2-459-photos.html. 15 April 2011

4. "Bobby Richardson," <u>Wikipedia</u>. Available at: http://en.wikipedia.org/wiki/Bobby_Richardson. 16 April 2011

5. "Draft lottery (1969)," <u>Wikipedia</u>. Available at: http://en.wikipedia.org/wiki/Draft_lottery_(1969). 25 April 2011

6. Asiado, Tel. "Jean-Paul Sartre, Existentialist Philosopher." Available at: http://www.suite101.com/content/jeanpaul-sartre-existentialist-a58399. 27 April 2011

7. "America's Navy A Global Force For Good." Available at: http://www.navy.com/. 3 May 2011

8. "Allen Hopkins (pool player)." <u>Wikipedia</u>. Available at: http://en.wikipedia.org/wiki/Allen_Hopkins_(pocket_billiards). 7 April 2012

9. "Jimmy Mataya," <u>Wikipedia</u>. Available at: http://en.wikipedia.org/wiki/Jimmy_Mataya. 29 June 2011

10. Hasson, LoreeJon. Personal Interview. 02 May, 2012

11. "Mike Massey," <u>Wikipedia</u>. Available at: http://en.wikipedia.org/wiki/Mike_Massey. 18 July 2011

12. Nankoo, Premanand. "Mike Massey Trick Shot Artist." Available at: http://eightballrack.com/mikemassey.html

13. Reid, Jimmy. "Professional Pool Player and Holder of More Than 40 Billiard Titles." Available at: http://www.freepoollessons.com/about_me.html. 18 July 2011

14. "George Frank Receives National Honor." Available at: http://www.bigskybusiness.com/index.php?option=com_content&view=article&id=627:george-frank-receives-national-honor&catid=29:montanabusiness&Iternid=29. 28 July 2011

15. "Young Adults Return Home After Marital Breakups." Available at: http://ns.umich.edu/htdocs/releases/story.php?id=1201. 13 August 2011

16. The Holy Bible. 1 Kings 3:16-28

17. "The Blizzard of 1996." Washington Weather. Available at: http://www.weatherbook.com/1996.htm. 7 April 2012

18. "Robin Bell Dodson - Pool Player, Hall of Famer, Businesswoman!" Available at: http://www.pro9.co.uk/html/print.php?sid+1711. 18 March 2012

19. Rossman, Tom "Dr. Cue" Personal Interview. 13 March 2012

20. "Meaning of Jayden - History and Origin." Available at: http://www.meaning-of-names.com/american-names/jayden.asp. 27 March 2012

17750665R00103

Made in the USA
Charleston, SC
26 February 2013